FORGIVENESS:
THE POWER AND
THE PUZZLES

FORGIVENESS:
THE POWER AND
THE PUZZLES

Wendell E. Miller

Wendell E Miller

ClearBrook*Publishers*

P.O. Box 1534

Warsaw, Indiana 46581

Forgiveness: The Power and the Puzzles

Unless otherwise indicated, the Scripture quotations in this book are from the New King James Version. © 1979, 1980, 1982, Thomas Nelson, Inc.

Scripture quotations marked (NIV) are taken from the Holy Bible, New International Version®. NIV®. © 1973, 1978, 1984 by International Bible Society. Used by permission of Zondervan Publishing House. All rights reserved.

Scripture quotations marked (NASB) are from the New American Standard Bible, © 1960, 1962, 1963, 1968, 1971, 1972, 1973, 1975, 1977 by The Lockman Foundation. Used by permission.

First Printing, May 1994
Second Printing, August 1994
Third Printing, January 2004
Fourth Printing, January 2006

Library of Congress Catalog Card Number 94-94384
ISBN: 0-9641-4410-7 paperback
ISBN: 0-9641-4411-5 hardcover
Printed in the United States of America

Dedication

To four godly women
through whom God has given me great blessings:

> *my dear mother, Florence Miller (with the Lord)*
> *my beloved wife, Lolita*
> *our two precious daughters, Cynthia and Candace*

Contents

Foreword

I would venture a guess that ninety-nine percent of the Christians alive today have never thought through the multi-faceted doctrine of forgiveness presented in *Forgiveness: The Power and the Puzzles*.

Though I have been a Christian for forty-eight years, have had twelve years of training for ministry in college, seminary, and graduate school, and have preached and taught the Word of God weekly for almost forty years, I have never discovered in my studies the marvelous program of forgiveness that Wendell Miller has discovered in God's Word.

How many have wrestled with the apparent conflict of instruction between Mark 11:25 and Luke 17:3? In the former, forgiveness is to be immediate and unconditional whereas in the latter it is conditioned by rebuke and repentance. These are two quite different instructions. But the differences don't stop there. A close study of Scripture reveals six different situations involving forgiveness. What a beautiful panorama is presented when they are all seen from their God-ordained perspective.

Truly, the inerrant Word of God demonstrates the absence of contradiction when we "study to show ourselves approved unto God, workmen who do not need to be ashamed, rightly dividing the Word of truth" (2 Tim. 2:15).

But this study not only demonstrates the doctrinal consistency of Scripture; it opens up and clarifies a way of success in exercising discipline and enjoying forgiveness and restoration to usefulness in the family of God.

I praise the Lord for the help I have received and I pray that multitudes will gain light and help from this careful study.

Earl D. Radmacher, Chancellor
Western Seminary

April 1994

Acknowledgments

I wish to acknowledge friends and associates who have provided help or encouragement. Some have shed light on a particular Bible verse or grammatical point and others have reviewed the entire manuscript. While only the author is responsible for the final results, all who have helped in any way have my deep appreciation.

Thank you

Steve Pulley enthusiastically entered into theological dialogue with me through several rewrites of the manuscript. Earl Radmacher has been a major contributor with his wisdom and selfless giving of his time.

A special word of appreciation is due Lehman Strauss, who read my manuscript as he traveled, and Jack Wyrtzen, who provided encouragement early in the project.

Many people have helped, more than I can list here, but the list includes: David Childs, Thomas Davis, Ivan French, Kittie Grill, Candace Howard, Lloyd Jonas, Cynthia Miller, Norman Olson, David Smith, Larry Thornton, and Terry Zolman.

My beloved wife labored alongside me, encouraging, and bringing clarity to my teachings by her questions.

Also, special thanks to my secretary, Helga Tess, whose many hours of typesetting, proofreading, and making creative suggestions are much appreciated. Any errors which remain are, of course, my responsibility.

Prologue

There is power in forgiveness—tremendous power. And yet, too often, forgiveness is powerless to help those who are hurting and who need it most. For some, forgiveness is powerless because they have not solved the puzzles of forgiveness.

The puzzles of forgiveness are like a jigsaw puzzle. A jigsaw puzzle must be solved as separate individual puzzles, one piece at a time. In like manner, understanding forgiveness is a larger puzzle that includes separate smaller puzzles.

In working jigsaw puzzles, sometimes a piece seems to fit where it does not belong, or it can be made to "fit" by forcibly pressing two pieces together. But then the puzzle cannot be solved completely—one piece is left without a "home." One piece must be discarded.

In solving the puzzles of forgiveness, some Bible teachers—even Bible teachers I respect and admire, from whom I have benefited greatly and to whom I will continue to look for insight into the Scriptures—have misplaced some pieces of the puzzle.

In misplacing these pieces, they failed to solve the puzzle of forgiveness. As a result of this failure, one of the most important pieces of the puzzle has been left without a home. And they have discarded this homeless but extremely important piece to the puzzle.

Without this important but discarded piece of the puzzle, the power of their forgiveness often fails. Just when this piece of the puzzle is needed most, just when using this piece of the puzzle is the biblical solution to their problem, they are left powerless— the piece they need has been discarded.

Should there appear to be any inconsistency in any of my solutions to the puzzles of forgiveness, the responsibility is mine. But to the extent that this study is a faithful reflection of biblical truth, the glory is God's who has taught me through His Holy Spirit and through various Bible teachers.

As you read this book, be "a Berean." Be willing to study and consider what I say, but do not take my word for anything. Instead, search the Scriptures to see if what I teach is biblical truth (Acts 17:11).

Because terminology used previously has proven to be inadequate to distinguish the various kinds of forgiveness clearly, I have introduced new terminology. If the terminology that I use should not be clear at any point in your study, please refer to Appendix A: "Definitions— Kinds of Forgiveness."

After you have solved the puzzles of forgiveness for yourself, you will have its tremendous power available, including the power to overcome "enemy" control of your life.

Of course it may be that your life is not controlled by your enemies *(or it may be— and you have not realized it)*. But you may know someone who needs the help taught in the chapter "Overcoming Enemy Control."

At times your problems may seem to be beyond the power of forgiveness. If that happens, you will lack the power to overcome enemy control of your life. Principles to extend the power of forgiveness to problems where forgiveness seems to fail are taught in the chapter "Extending the Power of Forgiveness."

Sometimes even the extended power of forgiveness "doesn't work." At those times, forgiveness that doesn't work is like children who get the pieces of one jigsaw puzzle mixed up with pieces of another puzzle. They are trying to solve a puzzle with the wrong pieces. A special chapter, entitled "When Forgiveness 'Doesn't Work,'" teaches biblical principles to use when you encounter such occasions.

What about the idea of "forgiving yourself"? Is it biblical? How does this idea fit with basic biblical principles of forgiveness? You may be surprised!

Or what about the idea that there are times when we should "forgive God"? Most likely you have heard or read something about this. This idea and several others are discussed in Appendix B: "Misunderstood— or Twisted and Mangled?"

Technical material is included in notes appended to the end of this book for those interested in studying the subject of forgiveness in more depth. You may want to ignore them. You don't need these notes to solve the puzzles or to have the power of forgiveness.

In a hurry? Need answers to the puzzles of forgiveness now? No time to study? A summary at the end of each chapter digests the teaching of that chapter. One solution would be to read these summaries, then come back to study each chapter as time permits.

But if possible, study each chapter until you have solved the problems of forgiveness, until you know the principles for overcoming enemy control, until you have the extended power of forgiveness, until you know what to do when forgiveness doesn't work, and until you have its quiet, life-changing power.

Solve the puzzles of forgiveness. Use its God-given healing power to help others, reconciling man with God, victoriously overcoming the offenses of others, healing marriage problems, restoring biblical parent-child relationships, promoting harmony in the church, and helping to equip the saints for every good work, all to the glory of God.

God has provided the power of forgiveness. Thank God and praise Him for His Word as you see the power of His principles and His Holy Spirit work in your life and in the lives of others.

Chapter One

Power, Puzzles,
and Fizzles

More than a celebration of independence, the Fourth of July meant noise to us. Oblivious of danger to fingers, eyes, or ears, we eagerly looked forward to shooting firecrackers. For some unexplained reason, boys like noise. The purpose of firecrackers is to make noise, and the more noise the better. As our ears rang after an explosion, they were trying to tell us that we were endangering our hearing. But to us, the greater the power of the firecracker, and the louder the "bang," the better.

Sometimes, after breathlessly awaiting a deafening explosion, fire merely shot out of one end of the firecracker. Instead of a bang, there was a hushed, rushing noise. With great disappointment we would moan, "It fizzled."

Forgiveness has tremendous power. It is energized by the power of God. It has power over many situations. Forgiveness has the power to reconcile sinners to a holy God. It has the power to overcome the offenses of others and to repair relationships that have been damaged. It has the power to overcome bitterness, anger, and wrath.

The power of forgiveness fizzles for two groups of people. The power of forgiveness fizzles for those who have not solved the puzzles of forgiveness. And it fizzles for those who refuse to use its power.

The puzzles of forgiveness, and the inability to solve those puzzles, have been evidenced in all civilizations. The conscience that God has placed in man's heart tells him he is guilty. The Word of God attests to this guilt. "All have sinned," and "there is none righteous, no, not one" (Rom. 3:10, 23).

Man has debated within himself, "I know I do some things that are wrong, but I'm really a good person. At least, I'm better than many others I know. I do many good things. Surely, God will give me credit for all the good I do. What additional works can I do to overcome the bad and tip the scales in my favor?"

God has given the answer in His Word. "No," God says, "you are not good. There is no one who does good. There is no good work you can do that can pay for your sins. By attempts to do what is right, neither you nor anyone else will be justified[1] *(declared righteous)*. Instead, the wages of sin is death. There is nothing you can do. Nothing!" (Rom. 3:10, 12, 23, 6:23; Gal. 2:16, paraphrased)

"But, because of My great love for you, I have given My Son, Jesus Christ, to die on the cross for your sins. He paid the price for your sins. He died in your place. The only way you can escape My righteous wrath is to accept My Son as your Savior" (John 3:16, 36; Rom. 5:8; 1 Cor. 15:3-4; Col. 1:20, paraphrased).

Instead of accepting what God says, man wants to find the remedy for sin in himself. This attempt is so universal that all of the religions of the world can be characterized by one word: "do"— do something to appease an angry god. In stark contrast, Christianity is not a religion of "do." Instead, it is "done"— Jesus did it all. He paid the price of our sins— He paid it all (John 19:30; Rom. 5:8; 2 Cor. 5:14). His death on the cross does *(for those who believe)* what no sinner could do for himself (John 3:16, 3:36; 1 Cor. 15:3-4).

The power of the forgiveness of sins is in Jesus' death on the cross. But this power is effective only for those who place their trust in His death on the cross by receiving Him as their Savior (John 1:12; Acts 16:31).

Let's consider the logic of God's plan for releasing *(freeing)* sinners from the penalty of their sins:

- God declares that all have sinned (Rom. 3:23).

- God also declares that the wages of sin is death (Rom. 6:23).

- By context, the death in Romans 6:23 is spiritual death— eternal separation from God.

- Therefore, since **all** are sinners, and the wages of sin is death, **all** must die spiritually— **all** must be separated from God for eternity.

- That is, **all** must die spiritually *(be eternally separated from God)* **unless** a substitute can be found who can die for **all** (1 Pet. 3:18).

Thus, forgiveness of sins is dependent upon having someone die for the sins of humanity. What are the requirements for this person? He must be sinless, or he would have to die for his own sins. In addition, this person must have sufficient value to pay for the sins of all humanity. Therefore, this someone must be infinite in value. This someone must be God. However, since God has life within Himself and cannot die, this person must also be man— a sinless man.

Jesus is God, but He also became the God-man as He took upon Himself a human body at the incarnation

(John 1:1, 14, 10:30). Because Jesus— God the Son— is infinite in value, took upon Himself a human body, and lived a sinless life on earth, He was able to die for all. And He did (2 Cor. 5:14-15). The idea of "for" is "in the place of." He who was sinless died on the cross, our sins being placed on Him (2 Cor. 5:21).

Let no one deceive you, appearing to honor Jesus by telling you that He is the best man who ever lived, while denying His deity (John 10:30). And let no one lead you away from your only hope by saying that He is the "way show-er." No! He is not the one who shows the way. He is the Way— the only Way (John 14:6)!

Appropriating the power of the forgiveness of sins is dependent upon a person's coming to Jesus as a helpless sinner, realizing his own helplessness, and knowing that no one will ever be released from the penalty of his sins by his own good works. Then, realizing that in his own strength he is both helpless and hopeless, he calls on God in the same desperate and trusting way a drowning person calls on a lifeguard to rescue him (Rom. 10:13; Gal. 3:11; Eph. 2:8-9).

Justification

Now let's look at God's plan for releasing people from the penalty of their sins as seen in the doctrine of justification. As taught in Romans 4:5, when a sinner puts his trust in what Jesus has done on the cross for him, that sinner's trust is accounted *("counted"— KJV)* for righteousness. That is, the payment that Jesus Christ made on the cross is **applied** to the trusting sinner's sins. The payment for his sins is **placed** onto his account even as a payment is made for a monetary debt.[2]

Then, with all of the trusting sinner's sins paid in full, God is able to maintain His absolute righteousness and yet declare this ungodly but trusting sinner to be judicially righteous (Rom. 4:5). That is, with all of the trusting sinner's sins paid in full, God declares him to be innocent *(from the penalty, not the fact)* of sin. Or to say the same thing another way, the trusting sinner is declared to be "positionally righteous" *(perfect in God's record even though in the sinner's experience he has sinned)*.

While sinners who are released *(freed)* from the penalty of their sins reap the marvelous benefits of forgiveness of their sins and justification *(being declared righteous)*, the **purpose** of justification is to satisfy God's righteousness. This purpose is explicitly stated in Romans 3:26— "that He *[God]* might be just and the justifier *[the one who declares righteous]* of the one who has faith in Jesus." After the blood of Jesus has been applied to the trusting sinner's sins, God is able, in all His holiness, to declare that trusting sinner to be judicially innocent.

Obviously, a trusting sinner— one who has been justified *(declared righteous)*— cannot be required by God to suffer the penalty of his sins. Instead of suffering God's righteous penalty for his sins, which is eternal separation from God, he has been released from that just penalty.

Initial Judicial Forgiveness

A basic meaning of "forgive" is "to release"[3-6] from some debt or penalty. As seen in the doctrine of justification, judicial forgiveness *(release from the penalty of sins)* is dependent upon two factors: (1) payment for sins that was made on the cross by Jesus Christ (1 Cor. 15:3-5); and (2) subsequent placement of this payment onto the account of the trusting sinner (Rom. 4:5; Col. 1:20-22). And, as taught explicitly in the Scriptures,

judicial forgiveness *(release)* from the penalty of sins
is made possible by the blood of Jesus Christ (Eph. 1:7;
Col. 1:14).

When a sinner puts his trust in what Jesus Christ
has done for him on the cross, he is reconciled to God.
Charles C. Ryrie says, "Reconciliation means a change
of relationship from hostility to harmony and peace
between two persons."[7] Narrowing the definition to that
of reconciliation of man with God, reconciliation is a
work of God in which, through the blood of Jesus Christ
on the cross, man is brought into a new relationship with
his Creator (Rom. 5:8-11; 2 Cor. 5:18-20; Col. 1:20-21;
Eph. 2:16).[8]

The fact that reconciliation *(new or changed relationship)* with God includes judicial forgiveness *(release
from the penalty)* of sin is seen in such truths as: "being
saved from wrath," "putting to death the enmity," and
"peace through the blood of His cross" (Rom. 5:9; Eph.
2:16; Col. 1:20-22).

The Holy Spirit through the Apostle Paul says, "Now
all things are of God, who has reconciled us to Himself
through Jesus Christ . . ." (2 Cor. 5:18). Surely, reconciliation must include **even more** than release from the
penalty of sin.

Initial Fellowship Forgiveness

Logically, reconciliation must include a change in
relationship in which fellowship with God, which was
broken by man's sins, is restored, reestablished, or
renewed. Just as man was created for fellowship with
God, and Adam had fellowship with God in the garden
of Eden, even so restoration of this fellowship must be
a part of this change in relationship that is called "reconciliation" (Gen. 3:8-24).

How does this restored fellowship relate to forgiveness? Recognizing that to forgive means "to release" from some debt or penalty, then, even as **release** from the penalty of our sin is judicial forgiveness, **release** from the alienation of fellowship *(that resulted from our sins)* is "fellowship forgiveness." One pastor teaches that the difference between these two kinds of forgiveness can be considered as the difference between God's "courtroom" and His "living room."[9]

While the Scriptures do not teach a doctrine that is called fellowship forgiveness, neither do they teach a doctrine called "the Trinity." And yet, the doctrine of the Trinity is crucial to our faith, and it is taught clearly in the Scriptures (Matt. 3:16-17; Mark 1:9-11; Luke 3:21-22; and John 14:16 with John 10:30).[10] Therefore, to understand biblical truth and to teach it to others, it is sometimes helpful to coin terminology that is not used in the Scriptures.

Before we put our trust in Christ and were justified, we were "alienated" from God by our "wicked works." But now He has "reconciled" us (Col. 1:21-22). Surely, reconciliation with God includes forgiveness that takes away alienation of fellowship caused by sin, and I call this fellowship forgiveness. Or, in the figure of God's living room, the sinner who has been reconciled is no longer restricted to the barn or back porch, but is now a welcome guest in the living room.

One Bible scholar says, "By reconciliation . . . fellowship with God is created."[11] This statement accurately reflects biblical truth. The Holy Spirit teaches restoration of fellowship with God in John's first epistle. John says, "Truly our fellowship is with the Father and with His Son Jesus Christ" (1 John 1:3b).

In addition, a restored fellowship with God can be seen in the fact that we are taught to come "boldly to the throne of grace" (Heb. 4:16). What greater proof of reestablished fellowship can there be than the fact that we can approach a holy God in prayer?

We can illustrate, by an example in human interpersonal relationships, the difference between God's judicial forgiveness *(release from the penalty of sin)* and God's fellowship forgiveness *(release from alienation of fellowship caused by sin)*.

If the boy next door threw a ball and broke one of the windows in your home, you might decide to release *(forgive)* him from the penalty of breaking your window. If so, you would be granting him judicial forgiveness— you would be releasing him from the penalty of paying to replace the broken glass.

But even though you released him from the penalty *(judicial forgiveness)* of paying for the broken window, you might choose not to release *(forgive)* him from the alienation that his offense caused. If so, even though you had granted him judicial forgiveness, you might ban him from playing in your yard.

Going back to man's relationship with God, we conclude that at the moment of saving faith God reconciles man to Himself— there is a complete change in relationship between God and the justified sinner. This complete change in relationship includes **two** kinds of forgiveness. Both pertain to sins committed up to the **moment** of saving faith:

- **Initial judicial forgiveness**— release from the penalty of sins committed up to the moment of saving faith

- **Initial fellowship forgiveness**— release from the alienation of fellowship caused by sins committed up to the moment of saving faith

Now we have **two** parts of the puzzle of forgiveness— two kinds of forgiveness that God grants at the moment a sinner places his trust in Jesus Christ. Figure 1-1 illustrates the two kinds of forgiveness that God grants at the moment of saving faith and justification.

In Figure 1-1, the vertical line, labeled "moment of saving faith and justification," is a time line, dividing this illustration into time prior to saving faith and justification, and time subsequent to justification. The arrow labeled "saving faith" and pointing up represents the admonition given by Paul and Silas to "believe on the Lord Jesus Christ" (Acts 16:31).

In response to saving faith, the blood of Jesus Christ is applied to all sins committed up to the moment of saving faith. The two arrows that point down illustrate the two kinds of forgiveness God grants as He responds to saving faith— initial judicial forgiveness and initial fellowship forgiveness.

As taught in this chapter and as illustrated in Figure 1-1, God grants both of these two kinds of forgiveness **at** the moment of saving faith and justification, and both pertain to sins **up to** the moment of saving faith and justification.

But what about judicial forgiveness for sins committed **after** saving faith and justification? And how is fellowship[12] with God affected by sins committed after saving faith and justification?

FORGIVENESS
AT THE MOMENT OF SAVING FAITH

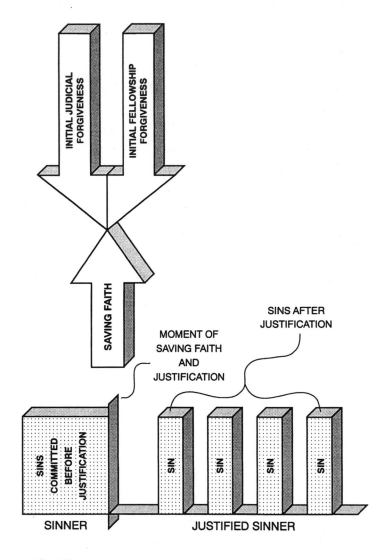

FIGURE 1-1

Summary

The religions of the world can be characterized by one word— "do"— do something to appease an angry god. In stark contrast, Christianity is not a religion of "do." Instead, it is "done"— Jesus did it all. Rather than vainly attempting to do some good works to appease God, the only way to eternal life is to trust the payment that Jesus made for our sins on the cross (John 3:16; 1 Cor. 15:3-4).

Let's consider the logic of God's way of releasing *(freeing)* sinners from the penalty of their sins. God declares that the wages of sin is death, and that all have sinned (Rom. 3:23, 6:23). It follows that all must die. That is, all must die unless a substitute can be found who can die for all.

This substitute must be sinless in his person and have sufficient value to pay for the sins of all humanity. This someone must be God. Jesus is God, He lived a sinless life, and He died for all (John 1:1, 10:30; 2 Cor. 5:21)!

Utilizing the power of the forgiveness of sins is dependent upon coming to Jesus as a helpless sinner— and calling upon God in the same way that a drowning person calls on a lifeguard to rescue him (Rom. 10:13; Gal. 3:11).

When a sinner puts his trust in what Jesus has done on the cross for him, that sinner's trust is accounted *("counted"— KJV)* for righteousness. That is, the payment made on the cross for his sins is applied to his account. With all of the sinner's sins paid in full, God is able to maintain His absolute holiness and yet declare this ungodly but trusting sinner to be judicially innocent. This is the doctrine of justification— God declaring ungodly sinners to be judicially innocent when they put their trust in the blood of Jesus Christ (Rom. 4:5).

Obviously, a sinner whom God can declare to be judicially innocent will not have to suffer for his sins. Instead of being required to suffer the penalty for his sins, the justified sinner is reconciled to God and brought into a new relationship with his Creator (Rom. 5:8-11; 2 Cor. 5:18-20; Col. 1:20-21; Eph. 2:16). Included in reconciliation are two kinds of forgiveness. **Both** pertain to sins committed **up to** the moment of saving faith:

- **Initial judicial forgiveness**

- **Initial fellowship forgiveness**

A basic meaning of "forgive" is "to release." Initial judicial forgiveness is release from the penalty of sins committed **up to** the moment of saving faith and justification; and initial fellowship forgiveness is release from the alienation of fellowship that was caused by sins committed **up to** the moment of saving faith and justification.

Now we have **two** parts of the puzzle of forgiveness— **two** kinds of forgiveness that God gives at the moment a sinner places his trust in Jesus Christ. But what about judicial forgiveness for sins committed **after** the moment of saving faith and justification? And how is fellowship with God affected by sins committed after saving faith and justification?

Chapter Two

What About Believers' Sins?

Early in Church history, some Christian leaders erroneously thought that baptism washed away sins. Even though they started with an erroneous idea, some of their subsequent reasoning was logical. They correctly questioned, "If baptism washes away my sins, what about sins that I commit after baptism?"

Then, not knowing what would cleanse them from the penalty of sins committed after baptism, they concluded that the way to keep from losing their salvation was to wait to be baptized until they were on their deathbeds.

Their plan was to drastically reduce the time between baptism *(which supposedly washed away their sins)* and the time of their death, thereby supposedly decreasing their chances of being lost because of sins they might commit after their "deathbed baptism." Some church leaders taught and earnestly recommended this plan.[1]

It is easy to see how, desperately hoping that they would not become lost again by sinning between the time of deathbed baptism and death, they arrived at an erroneous doctrine that has been taught through the centuries—the idea that sins come in two sizes, large and small. If committing "large sins" would cause them to become lost again, but committing "small sins" would not, there was reason to hope that they could avoid losing their salvation.

In the Catholic church, "large sins" have been called "mortal sins," and "small sins" have been called "venial sins." Some Protestants have followed the large sin— small sin idea. The large sin— small sin idea is reflected in the writings of various Christians who have referred to "our daily infirmities"— not realizing that our daily infirmities are included in the sins for which Jesus died.

What if someone were to say, "I haven't sinned in six years"? Wouldn't he in effect be saying: "I haven't committed a big sin for six years— I haven't killed anyone, committed adultery, robbed a bank, or committed any other really big sin in the past six years"?

Calling it one of the two greatest commandments, Jesus says, "You shall love the Lord your God with all your heart, with all your soul, and with all your mind" (Matt. 22:37). Could anyone possibly say that his every thought and every action has been an act of love toward God for any considerable period of time?

Obviously, the early church leaders who devised the deathbed baptism scheme did not understand God's provisions for sins they committed after placing their trust in the Gospel and being justified[2] *(declared righteous)*. Many Christians still do not understand.

This failure to understand God's provisions for sins committed after justification is, most likely, a root of legalism. If one could become lost again by committing large sins, but committing small sins would not result in becoming lost again, wouldn't you want someone to tell you where the boundaries are, lest you commit a big sin, fall off the edge, and be lost? Wouldn't you want someone to give you a list of the big sins?

It seems that some are saying, "Jesus died for my past sins, and He has saved me. Now, I am going to live the best life I can, and because I am going to live a good life, I will not become lost again." Are such people dividing sins into two categories—large and small? Are they saying that they will not become lost again because they are confident they will not commit any really big sins?

Can we become lost again after having been justified *(declared righteous)* by God? Let's look at it logically. Assuming that we could become lost again, and assuming that we do, who has failed? Have we? Or has God? Conversely, again assuming that we could become lost again, but we do not, who has kept us from becoming lost again? Have we? Or has God?

Consider man's logic: (1) God never fails, but man often does; (2) if our future sins could result in our becoming lost again, then we would have failed, not God; and (3) conversely, if we were to remain saved, then we would have kept our salvation by the way we lived. A preposterous conclusion!

Abandoning our own logic, let's look to the Scriptures. The Apostle Paul presents logic to show that if salvation is by grace through faith, then it cannot be by good works. He says:

- And if by grace, then it is no longer of works; otherwise grace is no longer grace.

- But if it is of works, it is no longer grace; otherwise work is no longer work (Rom. 11:6).

But is it possible to trust God for salvation through faith, and yet trust one's own good works to keep from becoming lost again (Eph. 2:8-9)? Paul answers this question in his letter to the Galatians: "Are you so foolish? Having begun in the Spirit, are you now being made perfect by the flesh?" (Gal. 3:3). Paul was saying, "You have been saved by faith; are you so foolish that you are now going to trust your good works?"

In our study of justification, we saw that when a sinner places his trust in what Jesus has done on the cross for him, payment that was made on the cross for his sins is applied to his account. Then, with all of his sins paid in full, God is able to declare the trusting sinner to be judicially perfect. But what about sins committed **after** the moment of saving faith and justification?

Repetitive Judicial Forgiveness

Those leaders in the early church who recommended deathbed baptism did not understand God's **three** provisions for judicial forgiveness for sins committed after justification. Many still do not understand.

One of God's three provisions for judicial forgiveness for sins committed after being justified— the **first** of His three provisions for continuing positional righteousness— is the sufficiency of the death of Jesus on the cross to pay for **all** sins forever. In Hebrews 10:12 we learn that Jesus "offered one sacrifice for sins forever," and Hebrews 10:14 teaches that this one offering of His blood "has perfected forever those who are being sanctified."

God's **second** provision for forgiveness for sins committed after the moment of saving faith and justification is a **High Priest**. As high priests in the Old Testament interceded for the people on the basis of the blood of animal sacrifices, Jesus, as our High Priest, intercedes for us on the basis of His shed blood.

However, there are two differences between the work of the priests in the Old Testament and our High Priest. One difference is that the blood presented by the priests of the Old Testament could never take away sins

(Heb. 10:11). Another difference is that, in the Old Testament, the office of each high priest was temporary.

Our High Priest is not like the priests of the Old Testament who had to be replaced as they died. Instead, since He never dies, Jesus has an "unchangeable priesthood" (Heb. 7:24). And He is able to "save to the uttermost those who come to God through Him, since He always lives to make intercession for them" (Heb. 7:25).

The fact that Jesus has a continuing ministry as High Priest, as taught in Hebrews 7:24, reveals a crucial truth. If His blood were applied to all of a trusting sinner's sins *(past, present, and future)* at the time of saving faith and justification, as some erroneously think, then believers would have no need for a High Priest. However, since Jesus is our continuing High Priest, we know that, at the time of saving faith and justification, His blood is applied **only** to sins committed **up to** that moment.

Further, as taught in Hebrews 7:25, being "saved to the uttermost" is inseparably connected to the truth that Jesus lives for the purpose of interceding. Again we can see that His blood was applied **only** to sins committed **up to** the moment of saving faith and justification.

Therefore, we conclude that, at the moment of saving faith and justification, God's judicial forgiveness for sins *(release from the penalty of sin)* pertains only to sins committed **up to** that moment— and judicial forgiveness for sins committed **after** being justified depends upon both the sufficiency of His shed blood and His intercessory work as High Priest.

Yes, He ever lives to intercede for us. By interceding on the basis of His shed blood, He can save us "to the uttermost" (Heb. 7:25). However, two crucial questions remain. Under what conditions will He intercede for us? And what must we do before He will intercede for us?

Thinking of 1 John 1:9, some would answer confidently, "I must confess my sins, and then He will intercede for me." But is this what God says? Others would
point to the teaching about advocacy in 1 John 2:1.

Referring to 1 John 2:1, it is clear that Jesus is our
Advocate. But how does His work of advocacy relate
to His work as Priest? Or is there any relationship? To
consider the relationship between His functions as Priest
and Advocate, it seems logical to consider three things:
(1) the person; (2) the work; and (3) the results.

Clearly, the Person *(Jesus Christ)* who is the High
Priest[3] of Hebrews 7:24-25 is the same Person who is
the Advocate in 1 John 2:1. What about His function?
Even as Old Testament priests interceded on the basis of
blood, Jesus died on the cross so that He would be able
to intercede on the basis of His shed blood. What about
results? The blood of bulls and goats both anticipated
and pictured the perfect sacrifice of the Lamb of God
so that the results are the same: judicial forgiveness—
release from the penalty of sin.

When speaking to a Jewish audience in the book
of Hebrews, God used a figure that the people understood— the priesthood. When writing to Gentiles, He
used a different word— "advocate." However, since the
Person, the work, and the results of the High Priest of
Hebrews and the Advocate of First John are identical,
we can confidently equate the two functions.

Advocate is not a word that we use commonly. What
is an advocate in the general sense? What is his role?
How does our Advocate of 1 John 2:1 function different-
ly than a secular advocate?

One Bible encyclopedia says, "The term *['advocate']* may be used technically for a lawyer. More
generally the word denotes one who acts in another's

behalf as a mediator, an intercessor . . . ."[4] In pre-Christian and extra-Christian literature, the Greek word that is translated advocate means "one who appears in another's behalf, mediator, intercessor, helper."[5]

In 1 John 2:1, we have an Advocate who intercedes for us with the Father. Our Advocate is Jesus. In this same verse, not only is Jesus identified as our Advocate, but He is called the Righteous One. Obviously, in God's courtroom, where all statements by our Advocate are absolutely righteous, He does not deny our sins, make excuses for us, plea bargain in our behalf, or try to have the case dismissed on the basis of technicalities.

Instead of attempting to obtain a believer's release from the penalty of his sins by denying his guilt or by presenting supposedly mitigating circumstances, every time a believer sins, Jesus identifies that believer as His own and says, "I paid for that sin on the cross, too." To that defense, there can be no other response but the one made possible by the cross. The Father answers, "That's right. We will mark it 'paid in full.' He is still judicially *(positionally)* perfect."

While advocate may seem like a strange word, other words fail to correctly convey the work of our Advocate. For instance, "lawyer" conveys the idea of attempting to prove innocence, and fails to picture the work of our Advocate. Rather than attempting to prove innocence, our Advocate admits our guilt and obtains our release from the penalty of our sins solely upon His merit— His sacrifice on the cross.

Other attempts to replace the word advocate, such as "one who speaks to the Father in our defense" also fall short (1 John 2:1 NIV). However, if we would be sure to remember that His blood is required for His work as

Advocate, and that the basis for His intercession is His blood, "Intercessor" might be a good word to use.

We have an Advocate. He is Jesus Christ. His function is to intercede on the basis of His shed blood. But under what conditions will He intercede for us with the Father? What must we do before He will intercede?

John answers these questions in his first epistle when he says, "If any saved person sins, that saved person has an Advocate with the Father, Jesus Christ the righteous" (1 John 2:1 paraphrased). Or, making the verse more personal, we paraphrase, "If *(whenever)* you sin, you automatically have an Advocate to intercede for you, and your Advocate is Jesus Christ the Righteous One."

Let's consider the words, "If you sin, you have an Advocate." The words before the comma state a condition, and the words after the comma state the results that follow the condition.

It is like a mother saying, "If you get into the mud and get your clothes dirty, you will get a spanking." Or she might say, "If you get into the mud and get your clothes dirty, **then** you will get a spanking." Notice that the results are the same, whether or not the results are introduced by the word "then."

Notice carefully: **if** you sin, you **have** an Advocate. You do not have to call your Advocate. He is on the job, interceding for you unconditionally whenever you sin, each and every time— even if you are not yet repentant, even if you have not yet confessed your sin, and even if you have not have realized that you have sinned.

Our Advocate is the **third** of God's gracious provisions for judicial forgiveness for sins committed after being justified. Have you thought of what this means?

Jesus intercedes for us upon the occasion of each new
sin, pleading our case on the basis of His shed blood,
without placing any conditions on us. Thus, God's judicial forgiveness of sins committed after justification is
unconditional. It is dependent **only** upon the faithfulness
of God—the One who always keeps His promises
(2 Tim. 2:13; Heb. 10:23).

Perhaps you are saying, "No, we must confess our
sins, and then He will forgive us our sins." If you do,
you are not alone. Many Christians believe that God's
judicial forgiveness of sins after justification is dependent upon confession.

The fact that judicial forgiveness of sins committed
after justification is **not** dependent upon confession
becomes clear when an apparent conflict between the
teachings of 1 John 1:9 and 1 John 2:1 is considered.
This apparent conflict is in the **conditions** that God
places on granting His forgiveness. In 1 John 2:1, His
forgiveness is unconditional, and in 1 John 1:9, His forgiveness is conditional *(dependent upon confession of
sins)*.

In considering this apparent conflict, some have
discovered the true relationship between 1 John 1:9 and
1 John 2:1. Others have come to one or more erroneous
interpretations.

One erroneous interpretation is that 1 John 1:9 speaks
of being saved from the penalty of sin. But being saved
from the penalty of sin is by faith (Eph. 2:8-9). Being
saved is variously described as "believing on the Lord
Jesus Christ," "receiving Him," and "calling on the
name of the Lord" (Acts 16:31; John 1:12; Rom. 10:13).
In stark contrast to this saving act of faith, being saved
from the penalty of sin is never taught as a result of confession of sins.[6] John includes himself in the teaching of

1 John 1:9, and we know that he was saved when he wrote this verse.

Out of this "salvation verse" misinterpretation of 1 John 1:9 comes a second error— the idea that, since Jesus intercedes for sins unconditionally after the moment of saving faith and justification (1 John 2:1), there is no need to confess sins.

Repetitive Fellowship Forgiveness

As taught previously, judicial forgiveness for sins committed after justification is **unconditional** with respect to man. That is, whenever you sin, you have an Advocate with the Father, and this Advocate is Jesus Christ the Righteous. Judicial forgiveness for sins committed after justification is entirely dependent upon the faithfulness of Jesus in interceding for every believer every time each believer sins (1 John 2:1).

Therefore, since the forgiveness in 1 John 1:9 is dependent upon confession of sins, and the forgiveness in 1 John 2:1 is unconditional, the "forgiveness" in these two verses must be **different**.

We have shown that God grants **two** kinds of forgiveness at the time of saving faith and justification— "judicial forgiveness" *(release from the penalty of sins),* and "fellowship forgiveness" *(release from alienation of fellowship that was caused by sins).*

Reason with me:

- Both judicial forgiveness and fellowship forgiveness for sins committed **before** justification are dependent *(conditional)* upon saving faith.

- Judicial forgiveness for sins committed **after** justification is unconditional (1 John 2:1).

- First John 1:9 teaches **some kind** of forgiveness that is **conditional** *(dependent upon a believer's confession of sins)*.

- Therefore, the forgiveness of 1 John 1:9 cannot be judicial forgiveness.

- Instead, the forgiveness of 1 John 1:9 must be fellowship forgiveness.

That is, God grants judicial forgiveness to believers unconditionally, as Jesus, our Advocate, intercedes for His own. In contrast, fellowship of believers with God, which has been broken by sin, is restored in response to *(dependent upon)* confession of sin (1 John 1:8-9).

Does the context of 1 John 1:9 verify this conclusion? Yes. Notice in 1 John 1:3, 6, and 7 that the subject is fellowship. Thus we confirm our conclusion that the forgiveness in 1 John 1:9 is fellowship forgiveness for sins committed **after** justification.

Now we have four pieces to the puzzle— four kinds of forgiveness that God grants. We can use our understanding of these four kinds of forgiveness to solve two more puzzles about forgiveness.

These are the **four** kinds of forgiveness that God grants:

- **Initial judicial forgiveness**— release from the penalty of sins committed before saving faith and justification—dependent upon faith in the Gospel as taught in 1 Corinthians 15:3-4

- **Initial fellowship forgiveness**— release from alienation of fellowship caused by sins committed before saving faith— also dependent upon faith in the Gospel

- **Repetitive judicial forgiveness**—release from the penalty of sins committed after saving faith and justification—unconditional *(dependent only upon the faithfulness of our Advocate, Jesus Christ, as taught in 1 John 2:1)*

- **Repetitive fellowship forgiveness**—release from alienation of fellowship caused by sins committed after saving faith and justification—dependent upon confession of sins, as taught in 1 John 1:9

Figure 2-1 includes the two kinds of forgiveness shown in Figure 1-1, and then adds the two kinds of forgiveness taught in this chapter—repetitive judicial forgiveness and repetitive fellowship forgiveness.

Praise God for the power of His forgiveness of sins. Praise Him for the power that resides in the death of His Son on the cross for you and for every believer. Praise Him for the power to release us from the penalty of sins, whether committed before or after the moment of saving faith and justification. Praise Him for the power to restore us to fellowship with Him, initially in response to saving faith, and thereafter to restore us to fellowship with Him in response to confession of sin.

A clear understanding of these four kinds of forgiveness will enable us to understand the puzzle of two other kinds of forgiveness— kinds of forgiveness that are God-given power for every believer— God-given power to overcome life's problems. His power of forgiveness will not fizzle.

———

FORGIVENESS THAT GOD GRANTS
FOUR KINDS

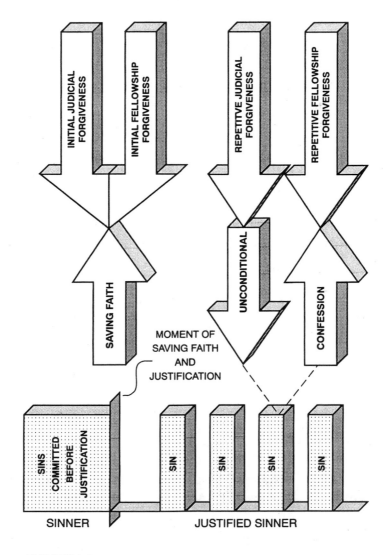

FIGURE 2-1

Summary

In chapter one we studied the **two** kinds of forgiveness that God grants **at the instant** of saving faith and justification:

- **Initial judicial forgiveness**— release from the penalty of sins committed **before** saving faith and justification— dependent upon saving faith

- **Initial fellowship forgiveness**— release from alienation of fellowship caused by sins committed **before** saving faith and justification— also dependent upon saving faith

But what provisions has God made for sins committed after justification? Some have sought the answer by erroneously trying to divide sins into two categories— "large sins" that will result in becoming lost again, and "small sins" that, supposedly, God can overlook.

If there were two categories of sins *(large and small)*, and if committing the large ones would result in becoming lost again, but committing the small ones would not, wouldn't you want someone to tell you which sins were the large ones, so that you could avoid falling over the edge and becoming lost again? Isn't legalism the logical result of not knowing God's provisions for sins committed after justification?

God's provisions for **judicial forgiveness** of sins committed **after** the moment of saving faith and justification include: (1) the sufficiency of the atonement; (2) the priesthood of Christ; and (3) **unconditional** intercession by Jesus our Advocate who intercedes for us with the Father.

In contrast, **fellowship forgiveness** of sins committed **after** the moment of saving faith and justification is

conditional. It is dependent upon our confession of our sins.

Thus, there are four kinds of forgiveness that God grants:

- **Initial judicial forgiveness**— release from the penalty of sins committed **before** saving faith and justification— dependent upon saving faith

- **Initial fellowship forgiveness**— release from alienation of fellowship caused by sins committed **before** saving faith and justification— also dependent upon saving faith

- **Repetitive judicial forgiveness**— release from the penalty of sins committed **after** saving faith and justification— unconditional *(dependent only upon the faithfulness of our Advocate, Jesus Christ)*

- **Repetitive fellowship forgiveness**— release from alienation of fellowship by sins committed **after** justification— dependent upon our confession of our sins

These four types of forgiveness provide the power of forgiveness of sins and fellowship with God. Praise God for His God-given power that will not "fizzle."

A clear understanding of these four types of forgiveness opens the door to understanding the puzzles and utilizing the power of two other types of forgiveness, power that God has given to every believer—power to overcome life's problems.

Chapter Three

If We Will, He Will

How many times have you prayed the Lord's Prayer? Hundreds of times? Thousands of times? Did you ever notice that you were putting a severe restriction on God's answer to your prayer?

Read this prayer again, and consider what you have been praying: "And forgive us our debts, as we forgive[1] our debtors" (Matt. 6:12). Doesn't this sound as if you have requested to be forgiven **only if** you forgive those who offend you—or to **the extent** that you forgive them?

Let's read two more verses on forgiveness: "For if you forgive men their trespasses, your heavenly Father will also forgive you. But if you do not forgive men their trespasses, neither will your Father forgive your trespasses" (Matt. 6:14-15).

Is God's forgiveness of us dependent upon our forgiveness of others? This would seem to be the case. What do you think? What does it mean when it says that our heavenly Father will not forgive us? In what sense will God not forgive us? If we do not forgive others, will we become lost again?

Possibly hoping that their unforgiveness of others is a "small sin" that would not result in becoming lost again, some Bible scholars have held the view that Jesus was saying that God would not forgive their "daily infirmities" if they did not forgive the offenses of others against them. However, our daily infirmities are not merely weaknesses. Rather, they are sins— sins for which the wages is death (Rom. 6:23). Our daily infirmities are included in the sins that sent Jesus to the cross!

What Will We Forfeit?

Of course, forfeiting forgiveness when we do not forgive others cannot mean that we will become lost again. Instead, our positional righteousness is secure in three gracious provisions of our heavenly Father: (1) the sufficiency of the Sacrifice (Heb. 10:12, 14); (2) a High Priest who never dies and who can save us to the uttermost (Heb. 7:24-25); and (3) an Advocate *(High Priest)* who intercedes for us upon the occasion of each and every sin— even before we confess our sins (1 John 2:1).

Well, you may ask, "If it does not mean that we will become lost again, what does it mean when we read that God will not forgive our sins?" Since, as we have seen in chapters one and two, God's forgiveness of believers includes both "judicial forgiveness" *(release from the penalty of sin)* and "fellowship forgiveness" *(release from alienation of fellowship caused by sin)*, it must be that we will forfeit God's "fellowship forgiveness" if we do not forgive others.

Therefore, we conclude that if we do not forgive others, our positional righteousness will not be affected. Judicially, we will remain perfect, even as we were at the moment we were justified. However, our fellowship with our heavenly Father will be hampered or perhaps even forfeited.

To say that our fellowship with God will merely be hampered may be minimizing the seriousness of disobeying God's command to forgive. And yet, it may be that believers, especially those who have not been taught biblical forgiveness, will not entirely forfeit God's fellowship by their failure to forgive. But, refusal to obey God in forgiveness, and the resultant damage to fellowship with God, should not be taken lightly.

To determine the forgiveness that we forfeit when we do not forgive others, consider the following:

- God grants believers **both** initial judicial forgiveness and initial fellowship forgiveness at the time of, and in response to, saving faith.

- God **maintains** every believer's judicial righteousness *(in spite of sins committed after saving faith and justification)* by repetitive judicial forgiveness that He grants unconditionally in response to the Advocacy of Jesus.

- Therefore, failure to forgive others **cannot** result in loss of judicial righteousness.

- Instead, the forgiveness that is forfeited must be God's **repetitive fellowship forgiveness** *(forgiveness that is also dependent upon confession of sins)*.

Recognizing that our fellowship with our heavenly Father will be hampered or perhaps even forfeited if we refuse to forgive others, what does this mean? Perhaps God will not hear our prayers[2] (Ps. 66:18). Or we may feel that God isn't there. Do either of these situations describe your relationship with your heavenly Father?

Perhaps someone is thinking, "Wait a minute, in the second chapter you taught that fellowship with God is restored by confessing sins" (1 John 1:9). True. Restoration to fellowship with God after committing a given sin is achieved by confessing that sin *(saying the same thing about it that God does)*.

What kind of fellowship do you think you would have with God if you confessed all of your other sins to God, but you **refused** to obey Him in forgiving others? If you stubbornly **rebel** against God, refusing to obey Him with regard to forgiving others, should you expect to be in fellowship with Him, even though you have confessed every other sin?

Because our fellowship with the Father depends upon our forgiveness of others, it is imperative that we know **how** to forgive others.

There are differing opinions on forgiving others— different interpretations of God's Word that are held by godly and scholarly believers. We need to know which interpretation is right.

Help from Supposed Contradictions

Sometimes one Bible passage seems to contradict another Bible passage. These supposed contradictions can be extremely helpful in determining truth if we are willing to let them. Apparent contradictions in the Scriptures should lead us to dig deeper and more carefully into His Word to see precisely what God is saying.

For instance, as we saw in chapter two, God's forgiveness of believers as taught in 1 John 1:9 is **conditional**. It is dependent upon confession of sins. In contrast, and in apparent contradiction, we saw in 1 John 2:1 that we have an Advocate, Jesus Christ, who intercedes for us unconditionally, every time we sin, providing judicial forgiveness that is **unconditional**.

By studying this apparent contradiction and the biblical context, we discovered that God grants **two kinds** of forgiveness to believers: repetitive judicial forgiveness, and repetitive fellowship forgiveness *(dependent upon confession of sins)*.

Conditional versus Unconditional

Jesus says, "Take heed to yourselves. If your brother sins against you, rebuke him; and if he repents, forgive him" (Luke 17:3).[3] Notice that the forgiveness in this verse is **conditional**— you are to grant forgiveness to those who offend you **if** and **when** they repent.

In contrast *(and in apparent contradiction)*, in Mark 11:25 believers are to forgive **unconditionally**. Jesus says, "And when ye stand praying, forgive, if ye have ought against any: that your Father also which is in heaven may forgive you your trespasses" (Mark 11:25 KJV). Or, in modern English, "And when you stand praying, forgive, if you have anything against anyone, that your Father who is in heaven may also forgive you your trespasses" (Mark 11:25, author's translation).

Just as in the biblical teaching of God's forgiveness of believers, in the teaching of our forgiveness of others we see apparent contradictions. In one Scripture passage, our forgiveness is to be **conditional** *(dependent upon repentance by our offender)*, and in another passage our forgiveness is to be **unconditional** *(repentance by the one who has offended us is not required)*.

What a striking parallel! Could it be that there are **two kinds** of forgiveness that believers grant? Could it be that these two kinds of forgiveness we can grant are similar to the two kinds of forgiveness that God grants us after we have been justified?

We have seen that different conditions *(conditional and unconditional)* distinguish the forgiveness of Mark 11:25 from that of Luke 17:3. But we can also find other differences between these two teachings on forgiveness.

Different Communications, Different Directions

In Mark 11:24, we see that the subject is prayer. Then in Mark 11:25, Jesus continues to teach about prayer. We notice that the forgiving of Mark 11:25 is accomplished **while** praying, and we can assume that it is accomplished **by praying**. In contrast, instead of being accomplished through prayer, the forgiveness of Luke 17:3 is accomplished **by speaking** to the offender— by responding to his repentance with the words, "Yes, I forgive you."

Considering again the difference in the means of communication *(prayer to God versus words spoken to an offender)*, the forgiveness of Mark 11:25 is a **vertical** transaction— between the offended person and God, and the forgiveness of Luke 17:3 is a **horizontal** transaction— between the offender and the one he offended.

Offender's Presence Not Required

Further, in Mark 11:25, where is the offender? And where is the repentance in Mark 11:25 that would make the offender eligible for the forgiveness of Luke 17:3? Neither the presence nor the repentance of the offender is required for the forgiveness of Mark 11:25. Instead, a believer is praying, perhaps with no one near him. The offender may be far away, and he may be unrepentant. But Jesus says, "Forgive." The forgiveness of Mark 11:25 **must** be different from the forgiveness of Luke 17:3.

Offender Not Forgiven

If you will read again the two translations of Mark 11:25 that were given above, neither one says "forgive **him**." This is because the word "him" is not in the

Greek New Testament.[4-6] Since we are instructed to
"pray and release" *(literal translation)*, instead of being told to "pray and release **him**," it seems logical to
believe that the omission of him by the Holy Spirit
is to help us see that the forgiveness of Mark 11:25 is a
different kind of forgiveness than the forgiveness of
Luke 17:3 in which the offender himself is forgiven.

Examining the Differences

Summarizing the arguments presented above, the
forgiveness of Mark 11:25 is different from the forgiveness of Luke 17:3 because:

- The conditions are different— unconditional forgiveness versus conditional forgiveness *(dependent upon repentance)*.

- The communications are different— prayer to
  God versus words spoken to the offender.

- The direction of the release is different— vertical
  release to God versus horizontal release granted to
  the offender.

- Neither the presence nor the repentance of the
  offender is required for the forgiveness of Mark
  11:25.

- Literally translated, Mark 11:25 says "forgive,"
  not "forgive him."

Thus, Mark 11:25 teaches a kind of forgiveness in
which we must, if we want to be obedient to God, pray
and unconditionally forgive *(even if the offender never
repents)* **whenever** we have anything against anyone.
Because this kind of forgiveness is upward in direction,
from man to God, we call it **vertical forgiveness**.

To Forgive Means to Release

If, in obedience to Jesus, I pray and forgive when the offender is neither in my presence nor repentant, what kind of forgiveness is this? Well, to forgive means **"to release"**[7] someone from something or **"to let off."** Since to forgive has the basic meaning to release or to let off, doesn't it seem logical that, in this forgiveness that is accomplished through prayer, we are releasing something or someone to God?

Release the Penalty of the Offense

But in vertical forgiveness, what are we releasing? Since Mark 11:25 says "forgive" rather than "forgive **him**," could it be that Mark 11:25 teaches unconditional forgiveness of the **penalty** of the offense and Luke 17:3 teaches conditional forgiveness of the **offender**? To gain an understanding of vertical forgiveness, first we must consider the moral basis for this kind of forgiveness.

Forgive? Or Get Even?

An offended person might **feel** as if he has the "right" to "get even" with an offender, and he might even erroneously **think** that he has such a right. However, the Scriptures teach that it is God's prerogative— not man's— to judge sin and to punish the wicked, because all sin is against God.

As David said, "Against You, You only, have I sinned . . ." (Ps. 51:4). And as we read in Romans, "Beloved, do not avenge yourselves, but rather give place to wrath; for it is written, 'Vengeance is Mine, I will repay,' says the Lord" (Rom. 12:19).

Have you ever thought about what it really means to get even with someone who has offended you? The one who has offended us is guilty before God. If you get

even with your offender, then you are guilty, too. Therefore, getting even means becoming equally guilty.

A Contract with God

Since God is the one who has the right to judge sin
and to punish the wicked, and since He has forgiven our
sins, it is reasonable for God to say, "I am the one who
has the right to judge sin, and I am the one who will
judge righteously. Release to Me whatever penalty you
might want to inflict on the one who has offended you."

Thus, the forgiveness of Mark 11:25 is an act of
obedience, accomplished through prayer, in which a
believer unconditionally releases to God his *(the offended believer's)* supposed right to get even. It is as if
a believer were thinking that he would like to get even
with someone who had offended him. Then, knowing
that he does not have a right to get even, *(in obedience
to the teaching of Mark 11:25)* he prays and unconditionally releases his supposed right to get even.

But how can an offended believer pray and release
something to God that already belongs to Him? No one
can forgive sins but God. The right to judge, to punish,
and to judicially forgive all belong to God.

When in obedience to Mark 11:25 an offended believer prays and releases his supposed right to get even,
he is **acknowledging** that it is God, not himself, who has
the right to judge, punish, and judicially forgive. He is
releasing to God the **penalty** of the offense that he *(the
offended believer)* might want to inflict on the offender.
He is **pledging** that he will not pursue vindictiveness.

Vertical forgiveness is an act of the will— a **commitment** or a **binding verbal contract**— made through
prayer, in which the offended believer commits himself
to avoid vindictiveness in action or word, or even in

wishful thought.[8] Having disarmed himself through the act of vertical forgiveness, he can treat the offender only in ways that are consistent with *agape* love.

Figure 3-1 illustrates vertical forgiveness. Someone, either a believer or an unbeliever, offends a believer. Whether the offender is repentant or unrepentant makes no difference.

The offended believer, seeking to please God and show God that he loves Him, prays and releases *(to God)* his supposed right to get even. While not shown in Figure 3-1, this means that the offended believer can henceforth treat the offender only in ways that are in accordance with *agape* love.

A Contract between Individuals

But what about the forgiveness of Luke 17:3? "Take heed to yourselves. If your brother sins against you, rebuke him; and if he repents, forgive him" (Luke 17:3). As shown above, this kind of forgiveness has to be different from the vertical forgiveness of Mark 11:25, because the forgiveness of Mark 11:25 is unconditional, whereas the forgiveness of Luke 17:3 is conditional. The forgiveness of Luke 17:3 is dependent upon the offender's repentance.

After a believer has prayed and unconditionally released the penalty of his offender's offense to God, in what sense does the offender need the conditional forgiveness of Luke 17:3? What is left to forgive? What does this forgiveness accomplish?

Since vertical forgiveness releases the offender from the **penalty** that the offender might want to inflict, the conditional forgiveness of Luke 17:3 must pertain in some way or other to release from **alienation** of the offender from the one he offended.

VERTICAL FORGIVENESS

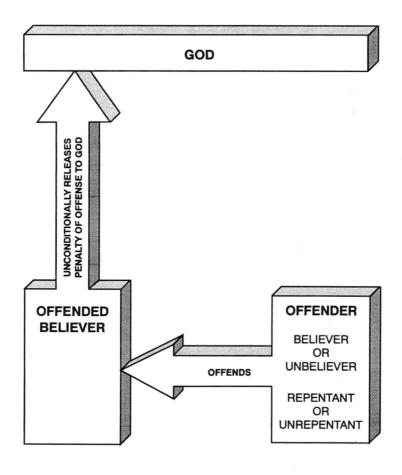

FIGURE 3-1

To distinguish the forgiveness of Luke 17:3 *(in which the offender is to be forgiven **if** and **when** he repents)* from vertical forgiveness *(in which believers unconditionally release to God their supposed right to get even)*, we call the forgiveness of Luke 17:3 **horizontal forgiveness**. This terminology reflects the fact that both the repentance and the granting of forgiveness are the work of humans.

Limitations of Horizontal Forgiveness

Since the purpose of horizontal forgiveness is to release an offender from alienation caused by his offense, it is logical that granting horizontal forgiveness to a repentant offender does not necessarily establish fellowship where none existed prior to the offense. Granting horizontal forgiveness to a repentant car thief does not necessarily make him my friend.

Less apparent is the fact that granting horizontal forgiveness to a repentant offender does not always, and sometimes cannot, reestablish fellowship to the level that existed prior to his offense. Some offenses damage relationships so seriously that it is impossible to reestablish fellowship to the degree that existed prior to the offense.

Striking Parallels

Notice the striking parallel between God's forgiveness of believers and man's forgiveness of others. God, in His gracious provision for continuing positional righteousness, releases *(forgives)* believers from the penalty of their sins unconditionally as Jesus pleads for sinning believers on the basis of His shed blood (Heb. 7:24-25, 10:12, 14; 1 John 2:1). In the same way that God forgives us **unconditionally**, time after time and day after day, God requires that we pray and release to

Him **unconditionally**, time after time and day after day, our supposed right to get even (Mark 11:25).

Notice another striking parallel. As believers who have been justified, we are restored to fellowship with God conditionally. We are restored to fellowship with Him **when** we confess our sins (1 John 1:9). In like manner, Luke 17:3 teaches that we are to grant horizontal forgiveness **conditionally** to those who offend us. We are to release them from the alienation that their offenses caused **when** they repent.

Their Dilemma

While I assume that nearly all readers will agree with the Bible teaching and simple logic set forth above, not all Bible students have held these views. Some theologians, who are both godly and scholarly, say that Mark 11:25 teaches that we are to have an attitude of forgiveness or a spirit of forgiveness and to be willing to forgive if our offenders should ever ask us to forgive them.

How can a clearly stated command to forgive merely mean "have an attitude of forgiveness" or "have a spirit of forgiveness" (Mark 11:25)? The **only** condition of Mark 11:25 is "**if** you have anything against anyone"[9] (author's translation).

Apparently these Bible scholars reason, "If the Scriptures really taught that I must forgive unconditionally *(without the necessity of the offender's repentance)*, then Mark 11:25 would be in conflict with its commandment that I must forgive *(conditionally)* **when** the offender repents" (Luke 17:4).

They seem to be confused about how they should act if they were to unconditionally forgive when the offender is unrepentant. This problem is worsened by what I believe to be erroneous definitions of forgiveness, such as "forgiving is acting as if I have forgotten" and "forgiving is never mentioning it again."

Those who use either of these erroneous definitions of forgiveness may be thinking, "If God were really teaching that I must forgive unconditionally, I could never mention the problem again, and then I could not obey God's teaching that I go to others and confront them and rebuke them for their offenses against me" (Matt. 18:15-16; Mark 11:25; Luke 17:3).[10]

And those holding the erroneous "never mention it again" definition may be thinking, "If Christians were to forgive everyone unconditionally, then church discipline would be impossible. We would never be able to follow the confrontation and church discipline procedures taught in Matthew 18:15-17."

Perhaps people holding this view would say, "We cannot unconditionally forgive those who have offended us, because we must be able to 'speak the truth in love' (Eph. 4:15). We must be able to say or do anything that is good for those who offend us."

Offender Not Forgiven

However, the problem disappears if the forgiveness of Mark 11:25 is correctly understood. In Mark 11:25, as a volitional act of prayer, a believer unconditionally releases *(to God)* his supposed right to get even. Or stated another way, he releases to God the penalty that he might want to inflict on the offender. Therefore, the forgiveness of Mark 11:25 has **nothing** to do with the offender *(except as it keeps the offended person's fist out of the offender's face)*. Instead, it is a verbal contract that the offended believer makes with God.

Unforgiven until He Repents

Thus it becomes evident that the offender **remains** unforgiven until he repents[11] (Luke 17:3). After praying and unconditionally releasing his supposed right to get even, the offended believer can say anything or do anything that is good for the offender. He can take any action to bring the offender to repentance, as long as it is in accordance with *agape* love.

As noted in the preceding paragraph, the offender remains unforgiven until he repents. But what about his offense? Are both the offender and his offense unforgiven until the offender repents? An example should be helpful in answering this question.

Mr. Black loaned money to Mr. Brown many years ago, and Mr. Black held a note specifying the amount of the loan. Finally Mr. Black became convinced that Mr. Brown could have paid him years ago, but Mr. Brown rebuffed all requests for payment.

As a believer, Mr. Black prayed and released to God the penalty that he felt like inflicting on Mr. Brown. But the offense still stood between them— Mr. Brown still had his money. Finally Mr. Brown repented, paid his note, and asked forgiveness for unfairly retaining Mr. Black's money. In response, Mr. Black released the note to Mr. Brown and released him from the alienation that his offense had caused.

From this example it can be seen that horizontal forgiveness **not only** releases the offense to the offender, **but also** releases the offender from the alienation caused by his offense. To release either one *(offense or offender)* is to release both. The Holy Spirit seems to speak alternately of releasing the offender and releasing the offense to the offender. Thus it makes little difference

HORIZONTAL FORGIVENESS

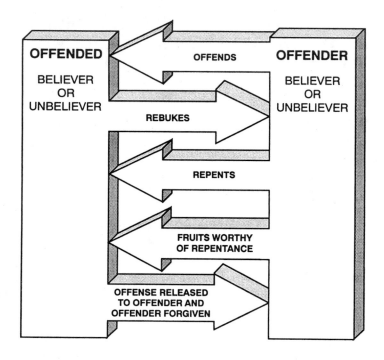

FIGURE 3-2

whether we speak of forgiving the offense or forgiving the offender.

Figure 3-2 illustrates horizontal forgiveness. Someone, either a believer or an unbeliever, offends another person *(believer or unbeliever)*. Biblically, the offended person rebukes the offender for the offender's good, with the goal of bringing the offender to repentance, using words that help the offender *(not corrupt words that destroy)*. When the offender repents *(if he ever does)*, making restitution *(fruits worthy of repentance)* if such is appropriate, the offended person releases the offense and grants horizontal forgiveness (Luke 3:8, 17:3, 19:8).

Vertical, Horizontal, or Both?

Earlier we saw that our fellowship with our heavenly Father depends on our forgiving when others offend us (Matt. 6:15). But does God's fellowship forgiveness of us depend on vertical forgiveness **or** does it depend upon horizontal forgiveness?

It is clear that our fellowship with God depends on vertical forgiveness. How do we know? Jesus, speaking of vertical forgiveness through prayer, says, "Forgive . . . that your Father also which is in heaven may forgive you your trespasses" (Mark 11:25 KJV).[12]

But is God's repetitive fellowship forgiveness in Matthew 6:12-15 dependent upon our use of vertical forgiveness or horizontal forgiveness? Consider two verses following the Lord's prayer: "For if you forgive men **their trespasses**, your heavenly Father will also forgive you. But if you do not forgive men **their trespasses**, neither will your Father forgive your trespasses" (Matt. 6:14-15).

Whereas Mark 11:25 teaches that God's repetitive fellowship forgiveness of us as believers depends upon

HORIZONTAL AND VERTICAL FORGIVENESS

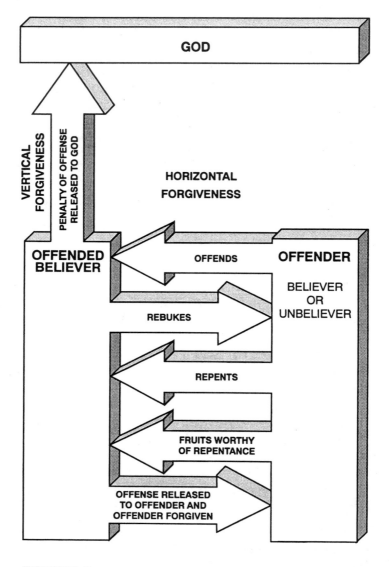

FIGURE 3-3

our obedience in using vertical forgiveness, it appears clear that these verses in Matthew teach that God's repetitive fellowship forgiveness of us **also** depends upon our obedience in using horizontal forgiveness.

How logical! If we were to obey God and use one of the two kinds of forgiveness, while stubbornly refusing to obey Him by using the other kind, how could we expect to receive His repetitive fellowship forgiveness?

Six Kinds of Forgiveness

In chapters one and two, four kinds of forgiveness were taught. All four are downward— God releasing man. In this chapter we have studied two more kinds of forgiveness, making a total of six that are taught in the Scriptures.

Vertical forgiveness is the fifth kind of forgiveness. As illustrated in Figures 3-1 and 3-3, vertical forgiveness is vertical in direction. It releases the penalty of the offense upward to God. The offended believer releases to God his *(the offended believer's)* supposed right to get even.

Horizontal forgiveness is the sixth kind of forgiveness. As illustrated in Figures 3-2 and 3-3, horizontal forgiveness is horizontal in direction— the offended person *(believer or unbeliever)* releasing the offense to the offender and releasing his offender from the alienation caused by the offender's offense.

With the discovery of vertical forgiveness and horizontal forgiveness, we have all six pieces to the puzzle of forgiveness.

Later we will consider how you can use the power of these fifth and sixth kinds of forgiveness, and how you should relate to offenders after using one or both of these kinds.

In the meantime, here is a thumbnail sketch of the uses of these last two kinds of forgiveness: vertical forgiveness is for the benefit of the one who forgives, and horizontal forgiveness is for the benefit of the offender who repents.

That is, offended believers who understand vertical forgiveness are not dependent upon the possibility that those who offend them might someday repent and ask for forgiveness. Instead, they have the power of vertical forgiveness.

It is helpful when offenders repent. But offended believers are not dependent upon the offender's repentance. It is not the offended person, but the offender, who needs horizonal forgiveness. The offender should feel guilty and want to be released from the alienation that his offense caused. But whether or not the offended person will grant horizontal forgiveness is between that person and God. When the offender repents and asks the offended person for horizontal forgiveness, he has done as God requires.

When you pray the Lord's prayer and ask to be forgiven as you have forgiven others, will your heavenly Father be able to grant you His repetitive fellowship forgiveness— to restore you to fellowship with Himself? If not, when you stand praying, forgive *(release to God the penalty of the offense to God through prayer)* if you have anything against anyone, and if any offender repents, forgive him, so that your heavenly Father will also forgive you your trespasses (Matt. 6:14-15; Mark 11:25; Luke 17:3).

If we will, He will. If we won't, He won't.

———

Summary

In chapter one we saw that God grants two kinds of forgiveness at the moment of saving faith and justification. One pertains to release from the penalty of sins, and the other pertains to release from the alienation of fellowship caused by the sinner's sins. Both of these kinds of forgiveness are **conditional**— dependent upon saving faith. **Both** pertain to sins committed **up to** the moment of saving faith:

- **Initial judicial forgiveness**— conditional *(dependent upon saving faith)*

- **Initial fellowship forgiveness**— conditional *(also dependent upon saving faith)*

Then in chapter two we learned that God grants **two more** kinds of forgiveness, and that these two kinds pertain to sins committed **after** the moment of saving faith and justification. The **third** is unconditional and pertains to release from the penalty of sins, while the **fourth** is conditional and pertains to release from the alienation of fellowship caused by the believer's sins:

- **Repetitive judicial forgiveness**— unconditional *(dependent only upon Jesus as our Advocate interceding for each and every sin)*

- **Repetitive fellowship forgiveness**— conditional *(dependent upon confession of sins)*

In this chapter we have seen that the Scriptures provide two more kinds of forgiveness, making a total of six kinds of forgiveness that are taught in the Scriptures. God has provided these final two for handling offenses between individuals:

- **Vertical forgiveness**— unconditional release to God through prayer of the offended believer's

supposed right to get even— release of the
penalty that he might want to inflict on the
offender

- **Horizontal forgiveness**— conditional *(dependent
  upon repentance of the offender)* release from
  alienation caused by the offender's offense

Vertical forgiveness is upward in direction— man
unconditionally *(without the necessity of the offender's
repentance)* releases to God whatever penalty he might
want to inflict, or might erroneously think that he has a
right to inflict, on the offender.

Horizontal forgiveness is horizontal in direction—
in response to the offender's repentance, the offended
person grants forgiveness to the offender— releasing
him from the alienation caused by his offense.

In this book, "judicial forgiveness" and "fellowship
forgiveness" refer exclusively to kinds of forgiveness
granted by God. Forgiveness in which believers unconditionally release to God their supposed right to get even
is called "vertical forgiveness," and forgiveness that one
person grants to an offender in response to the offender's
repentance is called "horizontal forgiveness."

Fellowship with God is dependent upon faithful
obedience to God's commands— practicing both vertical
forgiveness and horizontal forgiveness. Unless we obey
God, using vertical forgiveness whenever *(each and
every time)* we are offended, and unless we also grant
horizontal forgiveness when *(each and every time)* our
offenders repent: (1) our prayers may be hampered; (2)
we may not feel like praying; or (3) we may feel that
God is far away.

If we will, He will. If we won't, He won't!

Chapter Four

Forgive and What?

Forgive and forget. We hear these two words used together so often that we might wonder if they are twins. But are they? Is forgiveness inseparably connected to forgetting?

What about God's forgiveness? We know that God forgives sins, but does He forget them? If you believe that He forgets, you are in good company, because many godly Bible scholars believe and teach that He does. But is it really true? Has anyone shown you where the Bible teaches that God forgets sins?[1-2]

Why, in a study of forgiveness, should we be concerned with whether or not God forgets sins? Well, if God really "forgives and forgets," perhaps He expects us to do the same. If we forgive but do not forget, is there something wrong with our Christian walk? If the two go together and we do not forget, have we really forgiven?

This may not be a problem to you, but many, many Christians have trouble believing that they have really forgiven when they remember the offense. They become hurt or angry when they remember the offense, so they think they have not forgiven. Thus it is important to consider whether or not God forgets sins.

Through the prophet Jeremiah, God says, "I will forgive their iniquity, and their sin I will remember no more" (Jer. 31:34). What does it mean, "I will remember their sin no more"? Does not remembering necessarily mean forgetting? If it doesn't mean forgetting, what does it mean?

Context Determines Word Meaning

Some words, whether used in the Bible or in secular society, carry distinctly different meanings when used in different contexts, and the meaning can best be understood from the context. For example, hopefully you will agree that salvation is by grace, through faith, and not of works. However, the Bible also reports that Paul and his shipmates could not be saved unless they stayed with the ship (Acts 27:31). Obviously, as seen in the context, "saved" means being saved from drowning.

Or consider another example. Does the Bible teach that only after Joseph and Mary were married, after they had taken a long and tiring journey together to Bethlehem, and after the birth of Jesus, Joseph was introduced to Mary? The Bible says that Joseph "did not know her till she had brought forth her firstborn Son . . ." (Matt. 1:25). No, the phrase "did not know her" is not referring to the meeting of someone— it is speaking of the fact that a husband-wife physical relationship did not exist between them before Jesus was born.

Remembering and Forgetting

So often we stumble over the meaning of biblical words even if we use these words precisely the same way in our culture. Imagine that your name is Jack and that you have a rich uncle. One day you are talking with your elderly uncle. "Uncle Bill, I would like to be remembered in your will."

Uncle Bill replies, "Jack, I am seeing my lawyer next week, and I have been planning to do that very thing."

Sometime later Uncle Bill dies, and his attorney calls all the relatives and heirs into his office. As the lawyer reads the will, you hear, "—and to my nephew Jack, who asked to be remembered in my will—" The lawyer hesitates, then continues, "Hello, Jack, I remember you. How are you doing?"

It is doubtful that anyone would think that "remembering in a will" means "thinking about." Conversely, it is doubtful that anyone would think that not being remembered in a will meant that the deceased had forgotten the fact of a certain person's existence. And yet, when the Bible says that God will "remember no more," many Christians have no idea that it could mean anything other than forgetting.

The thief on the cross said to Jesus, "Lord, remember me when You come into Your kingdom" (Luke 23:42). Let's try equating remembering with not forgetting in this account of the thief on the cross. Do you suppose that the thief on the cross was asking Jesus to think about him after he had died and gone to hell?

Of course, this interpretation of remember is ridiculous. The thief wanted to be remembered in blessing. He asked to be remembered when Jesus came into His kingdom, and he received the blessing of glorification: "Assuredly, I say to you, today you will be with Me in Paradise" (Luke 23:43).

As illustrated above, to remember, when used in the Scriptures, often means to remember in blessing or vengeance. Conversely, to not remember often means to not remember in blessing or vengeance.

One of the most important truths in the world is that God will not remember our sins against us. Because Jesus has both paid for and forgiven all of the sins of every believer, God cannot remember our sins against us in vengeance. Paul teaches this beautiful truth when he says, "There is therefore now no condemnation to those who are in Christ Jesus . . ." (Rom. 8:1).

He Knows Everything

One of the attributes of God is that He knows everything. There is nothing past, present, or future that He does not know. If He knows everything, and He does, what has He forgotten? Of course, the answer is that He has forgotten nothing. Thus we conclude that His forgiveness of sins has nothing to do with forgetting that we have sinned or any of the facts relating to our sins— but that He will not remember our sins against us.

Consider this imaginary scene: in making my point, I hope that I will not appear to be blasphemous. One day in eternity you are talking to God, and you say, "I was wondering about David's sin with Bathsheba." God replies, "Did David sin? I don't remember that. I must have forgotten." Ridiculous, isn't it, that God would not know what He had written in His own Word (2 Sam. 11)? And yet, it seems that everywhere we turn, Christians are taught— and believe— that God forgets sins.

Or consider this: a Sunday school class is in session, and the lesson is about Ananias and Sapphira. The Scriptures are read, and there is discussion about the text. It is hard to believe that God would have no knowledge of the fact of sins committed when He hears them read and discussed all over the world week by week (Job 34:21-22; Acts 5:1-11).

"Forgetting" in the Bible

The Bible does use the word forget, and this word is used in various senses. Although word studies in the original languages are important, we can learn much about the sense in which a word is used by considering the context. As we will show in the following paragraphs, this is true with the word "forget."[3-5]

For instance, forget is used in the sense of neglecting to do some task. Mark's Gospel tells us: "Now the disciples had forgotten to take bread . . ." (Mark 8:14). Their forgetfulness was not permanent. Jesus warned about the leaven of the Pharisees, and immediately they remembered that they had not packed a lunch.

James expresses a similarity between "doing" and "not forgetting." He says, "But he who looks into the perfect law of liberty and continues in it, and is not a forgetful hearer but a doer of the work, this one will be blessed in what he does" (James 1:25).

In Hebrews we read, "For God is not unjust to forget your work and labor of love which you have shown toward His name, in that you have ministered to the saints, and do minister" (Heb. 6:10). Here not forgetting refers to not neglecting to reward believers for their Christian service.

The chief butler to Pharaoh had been released from prison and had been restored to his former service with Pharaoh even as Joseph had prophesied. Most likely at various times the chief butler would think, "I must do something to reward Joseph." And yet he neglected to put his good intentions into action. The Scriptures say, "Yet the chief butler did not remember Joseph, but forgot him" (Gen. 40:23).

Here not remembering is used in the sense of not remembering in blessing. And in the same verse, forgetting is used in a similar sense— neglecting to reward someone.

Sometimes forgetting is used to convey the idea that God delays in answering prayer. The Psalmist asks God: "How long, O LORD? Will You forget me forever? How long will you hide Your face from me?" (Ps. 13:1)

"Has God forgotten to be gracious? Has He in anger shut up His tender mercies? Selah" (Ps. 77:9). Notice that this forgetting is an intentional withholding of blessing, and has nothing to do with a slipping of the memory, a temporary lapse of memory, or a complete loss of the memory of a fact.

Jeremiah the prophet, quoting God's pronouncement of judgment, said, "Therefore behold, I, even I, will utterly forget you and forsake you, and the city that I gave you and your fathers, and will cast you out of My presence. And I will bring an everlasting reproach upon you, and a perpetual shame, which shall not be forgotten" (Jer. 23:39-40).

These verses in Jeremiah are speaking of God as if He forgets in the sense of removing His blessing. Consider the following logic: (1) God is going to bring "an everlasting reproach and an everlasting shame" to a people; (2) others will know and speak of this "everlasting reproach" and "perpetual shame"; (3) God knows every thought and every word of everyone; and yet (4) God will forget these people who are a "shame and everlasting reproach."

That is, God will forget them in the sense of not blessing them. This withholding of His blessing will be so complete that He will forsake them. But He will know the facts of their sins along with their "everlasting re-proach" and "perpetual shame."

The Psalmist says of the wicked: "He has said in his heart, 'God has forgotten; He hides His face; He will never see'" (Ps. 10:11). They try to convince themselves that God has forgotten. Many godly Bible scholars teach that God forgets sins, and they are not alone. God says that the wicked also try to convince themselves of God's forgetfulness.

No Example of Forgetfulness

If you agree that God does not forgive and forget, then He has **not** given you an example of forgetfulness to follow. So why try?

Nowhere in the Scriptures has God provided an example in which He has forgotten any fact. He knows the stars by name, knows the number of hairs on our heads, and knows every thought, every action, and every sin of everyone, saved and unsaved. He does not forget the fact of our sins. Instead, we have the blessed truth that, although He has not forgotten them, He will not remember them in vengeance against believers. Jesus paid it all.

It is unfortunate that the misconception prevails that God's forgiveness is accompanied by an intentional loss of memory, because it is likely that this erroneous idea has given birth to the commonly-held misconception that believers must do the **impossible**— forgive and forget. It is **not** in your power to forget anything volitionally. Some things may slip your mind, but you **cannot** erase them from your memory as an act of the will.

The Apostle Paul chose to strip the past of power to control his actions in the present by "forgetting" what was behind (Phil. 3:13). It is beyond imagination to think that Paul ever forgot his part in the stoning of Stephen or his persecution of the Church (Acts 6:5-8:1). We know that he remembered what he had done in the past, because he rehearsed some of it on various occasions (Acts 22:4-7, 26:11-15; 1 Cor. 15:9; Gal. 1:13; Phil. 3:6). But he volitionally and resolutely determined that he would not allow the past to keep him from glorifying God in the present.

Why Try the Impossible?

Have you tried to forgive and forget, only to find that you cannot forget? The more determined you are to forget, the more firmly a fact becomes entrenched in your mind. Have feelings of hurt or anger ever come back after you thought that you had forgiven? Because you remembered the offense, or because this remembrance still caused you pain, did you doubt that you had forgiven? Did you wonder if you would ever be able to forgive?

Obey God—and Be Free

Rejoice! There is hope! God has not asked us to do the impossible— He has not commanded that we forget the offenses of those who have hurt us. He knows that we cannot, as an act of the will, forget anything. Instead of commanding the impossible, He has given us the gift of **vertical forgiveness**. He commands that we use this power by praying and releasing the **penalty** of each offense against us. That we can do, and we must. We cannot forget them, nor should we try!

Our all-knowing God has given us the power of vertical forgiveness as a loving gift. Obey God: use the power of vertical forgiveness— pray and unconditionally release to Him the penalty of each offense whenever you have anything against anyone.

Obey God: **use** the power of horizontal forgiveness—grant forgiveness when your offender repents. Use it primarily for the good of the offender.

If you are the offender, **ask** the one you offended to forgive you. If the one you offended is not a believer, does not know about the power of vertical forgiveness, or refuses to avail himself of this power, you may be able to help him by asking him to forgive you.

If you are the one who has been offended, graciously grant horizontal forgiveness **as soon as** the offender repents. He needs to have the burden of his offense lifted.

Remember, as an offended believer, you **always** have the power of vertical forgiveness: you are **not** dependent upon horizontal forgiveness. Whether your offender repents or not has **no** effect on the God-given power of vertical forgiveness.

Forgive and forget? The idea of forgive and forget presents not only an unbiblical concept, but also presents an unworkable plan— a burden that God has not placed on us— a task that is impossible to accomplish. To attempt to forget makes one a slave of his own memory. His memory of the past becomes his master, tyrannically ruling over him. In wonderful contrast, there is power in forgiveness. Use the power of vertical forgiveness. Forgive— forgive and be free. **Be free** from the power of painful, life-dominating memories.

———

Summary

Forgive and what? If God "forgives and forgets," perhaps He requires that we do the same. However, if God forgives but does not forget, then His actions have not provided an example of forgetting for us to follow.

In nearly **all** instances, the memory of an offense remains after forgiving. This is true when vertical forgiveness is used to unconditionally forgive *(release to God)* the penalty of an offense of another, and it is true when horizontal forgiveness is used to conditionally forgive a repentant offender. And it is **not** unusual for hurt feelings or anger to remain also. Unfortunately, when hurt feelings or anger remain after forgiving, many Christians think that they have not forgiven.

Or they are convinced that they are unable to forgive. Then they feel hopelessly unable to deal with the offense, the offender, and their feelings.

The idea that God forgets sins seems to come primarily from a misunderstanding of the word "remember." God will not "remember" our sins in vengeance. But "not remembering" has nothing to do with God's knowledge of the facts of our sins.

Further, forget is used in various senses in the Bible, such as neglecting to do a task, or withholding a blessing. But the Scriptures do not teach that God forgets the fact that we have sinned.

Since God does **not** forget our sins, we do **not** have an example of forgetting to follow. God does not forget, and He does not expect us to forget offenses against us. Don't even try to forget. It is impossible to forget anything as an act of the will.

Use the power of vertical forgiveness, unconditionally releasing to God the penalties of your offender's offenses. And, as you have opportunity, use the power of horizontal forgiveness to help your offender. If you are the offender, ask the one whom you offended for forgiveness. If you are the offended person, grant horizontal forgiveness as soon as your offender repents. But, as a believer, you are not dependent upon his repentance. You have the power of vertical forgiveness through prayer.

Forgive as the Scriptures command, but don't **even try** to forget. Use the power of vertical forgiveness and be free. Forgive and **be free** from the power of painful memories.

Chapter Five

Why Forgive?

You are alone in your room. Suddenly, surrounded by a blazing light, God appears in your room. God says, "You are holding an offense against Joe. Turn the penalty of that offense over to Me. Do it now. That is an order!" Would you obey?

What if God sent you a telegram commanding that you turn over to Him the penalty of an offense? Would you obey?

I doubt that He will appear in a blaze of light or send a telegram, but He has commanded in His Word that you pray and unconditionally forgive whenever you are holding anything against anyone (Mark 11:25). Will you obey?

Remember, when you use vertical forgiveness, by means of prayer, you unconditionally *(even without the offender's repentance)* release to God the penalty of the offense. In praying and releasing to God the **penalty** of the offense, you are **not** forgiving the offender. He still needs your forgiveness. Instead of forgiving him, you are turning over to God, for His judgment, the **penalty** of his offense.

Why use vertical forgiveness? One reason should be sufficient, but there are at least eleven biblical reasons to use vertical forgiveness— and we will consider all eleven.

Obedience

Obeying a direct command of God is the first and most important reason to pray and unconditionally forgive. Without even considering any other reasons, obedience to God should be a sufficient reason to pray and release to God the penalty of the offense.

Loving God

But consider some other reasons. Jesus says, "If you love Me, keep My commandments" (John 14:15). This is our second reason to use vertical forgiveness. If we obey His commandment, we are loving God. Holding onto the penalty of an offense means not loving God enough to obey Him.

Fellowship with God

Would it make sense to let anyone keep you out of fellowship with God? If you do not pray and unconditionally release to God the penalty of every offense, your fellowship with God will be hampered. Jesus says that you must unconditionally forgive— so that your heavenly Father may forgive you your trespasses (Mark 11:25). This is a third reason to release to God the penalty of every offense.

Power in Prayer

Suppose that someone hit you in the nose. You had not offended him— he just thought it would be fun to hit you. As you stood with a throbbing, bleeding nose, he laughed at you.

Would you want the person who hit you to keep you out of fellowship with God? Would that be the wise thing to do? Or would wisdom dictate that you use vertical forgiveness— and be in fellowship with God? Could it be that you are out of fellowship with God because of your refusal to pray and unconditionally release to God the penalty of each offense?

God says that you must pray and unconditionally forgive *(release to God the penalty of the offense)*. If you do not, you will be out of fellowship with God because of your disobedience.

Frequently a counselee who has not used vertical forgiveness will tell me it seems God is far away. I tell the counselee that most likely God is not hearing his prayers (Ps. 66:18). Peter teaches that prayers can be hindered (1 Pet. 3:7).

One result of being out of fellowship with God may be powerlessness in prayer. Avoiding this condition is a fourth biblical reason to use vertical forgiveness (Mark 11:25 and Matt. 6:15).

All Offenses Are against God

Consider another biblical reason to use vertical forgiveness: It is your nose that caught a fist, and it is your nose that is throbbing and bleeding, but the sin is **not** really against you. It is against God (Acts 5:3-4).

King David said, "Against You, You only, have I sinned, and done this evil in Your sight . . ." (Ps. 51:4). From a human standpoint, it would seem that David sinned against Bathsheba and her husband, but from God's standpoint, the sin was against Him. As Creator of the world, God has the right to determine right and wrong; all transgressions of His moral law are sins against Him. This is our fifth reason to use vertical forgiveness.

Therefore, when you pray and turn over to God the penalty of an offense, tell God that you know that the offense was really against Him, and not against you. Sure, it is your nose that hurts, but the person who struck you has defied the living God in the way he treated you.

God Will Judge and Punish Offenders

Imagine that you are a little kid. A big bully has beaten you up, and you have gone home crying. Your big brother says, "Who did this to you? I'll take care of him."

That is what God is saying: "Turn it over to Me. I will take care of it." As the Scriptures say, "Beloved, do not avenge yourselves, but rather give place to wrath; for it is written, 'Vengeance is Mine, I will repay,' says the Lord" (Rom. 12:19). This is a sixth reason to use vertical forgiveness.

God's Justice Includes Believers' Offenses

But what about the believer who has offended you? We know that God cannot take vengeance on believers because "there is therefore now no condemnation to those who are in Christ Jesus" (Rom. 8:1).

However, as taught in chapter four, God does not forget anything. He will not forget how a believer has treated you. Some Bible students believe that, at the judgment seat of Christ, either God will bring up the offenses of others who have offended you, or that your offenders will give account of themselves to God, confessing how they have offended you. The Scriptures do teach accountability (Matt. 12:36; Rom. 14:10-12; 2 Cor. 5:10; Heb. 13:17; 1 Pet. 4:5). If there is no accountability, why does the Apostle Paul speak of living the Christian life with "fear and trembling" (Phil. 2:12)?

Whether or not a believer will suffer humiliation at the judgment seat of Christ, and whether or not he loses rewards because he has offended you, is God's business (1 Cor. 3:11-15, 4:5). Jesus died for your sins, and He died for the sins of the believer who has offended you. With the believing offender's debt paid in full on the cross, justice has been done. Pray and unconditionally release to God the penalty of the offense, as He commands. This is our seventh reason.

Thus far we have seen seven reasons why we should use vertical forgiveness whenever we are offended by anyone:

- Doing so is obeying a command of God.

- Obeying God in vertical forgiveness is one way to love Him.

- Obeying God in vertical forgiveness maintains fellowship with God.

- Obeying God in vertical forgiveness maintains power in prayer.

- Offenses against you are really against God. *(It is God's right to get even, not ours.)*

- God will judge and punish offenders.

- Jesus died for the sins of those who offend us. *(Justice has been done.)*

In addition to these seven biblical reasons to use vertical forgiveness, there are at least four more.

God Has Forgiven Us

Ephesians 4:32 teaches that we are to "be kind to one another, tender-hearted, forgiving each other, just as God in Christ also has forgiven *[us]*" (NASB). Because God has forgiven us, we are to forgive. Whether we consider it an obligation *(which it is)* to forgive because He has forgiven us, or whether we do it out of love and gratitude for His forgiveness of our sins, our eighth reason to use vertical forgiveness is that He has forgiven us.

God Has Forgiven Us More

A certain king was going to take account of his servants (Matt. 18:23-24). One of his servants was not an ordinary servant. He had a special relationship to the king— much like an executive assistant today.

Perhaps this servant was in charge of collecting the rent from tenant farmers over a wide area of the king's holdings. Somehow he had come up short— very short — in the money that he should have had. Just assume that his debt was several lifetimes of his wages. That is the gist of the events that Jesus was recounting— the servant owed a debt that he could never pay.

In the account of Matthew 18, the king forgave his servant a debt that the servant could never have paid. In like manner God has forgiven us a debt so large that we could never repay.

As pictured in this illustration, God has forgiven us **much more** than others could ever offend us. This is a ninth reason to use vertical forgiveness.

God Has Forgiven Us Unconditionally

The king knew that there was no possibility of ever getting his money back, so he commanded that the servant, his wife, his children, and all that he had be sold into slavery (Matt. 18:25). Then, after receiving a pittance in comparison to the debt owed him, the king would have to write off the remainder of the servant's debt.

The servant was desperate! He, his wife, and all of his children were to be sold into slavery! A desperate person will grasp at any straw— and this one did.

From a logical standpoint, he did a very foolish thing— he asked for time to repay a debt that he could not possibly have paid in several lifetimes (Matt. 18:26). Notice carefully, he asked for more time to repay. He didn't ask to be forgiven.

Surprisingly, even though the servant did not ask to be forgiven, the king had compassion on him and forgave him his enormous debt (Matt. 18:27).

What does this tell us? The illustration is about forgiveness, and Jesus has given this illustration to teach spiritual truth. What spiritual truth? The servant pleaded for more time to repay. He didn't ask to be forgiven. The king forgave him unconditionally.

Does the king's forgiveness of his servant picture initial judicial forgiveness— God's forgiveness of us at the time of justification? No. God's forgiveness of sinners at the time of justification is conditional. It is dependent on the sinner's saving faith. In sharp contrast, the king forgave his servant unconditionally.

But what about God's repetitive judicial forgiveness of believers' sins *(sins committed after saving faith and justification)*? It is unconditional.

The illustration that Jesus used teaches that, because God's forgiveness of our sins is unconditional, when we are offended by others, our forgiveness must also be unconditional. Even as we have been forgiven unconditionally, time after time, we are to forgive unconditionally *(vertical forgiveness)*.[1]

The huge debt that the servant could not pay no doubt included many financial losses, but even one of the sins we commit after saving faith and justification is a debt that we could never repay. Again we see that the illustration of Matthew 18 portrays the blessed spiritual truth that God unconditionally grants us His repetitive judicial forgiveness every time we commit a sin after the moment of our saving faith and justification.

Because God forgives our sins unconditionally, we are to unconditionally release to God the penalty of every offense against us. This is a tenth reason to use vertical forgiveness.

Avoiding Chastisement

In the same illustration, a fellow servant owed the forgiven servant a pittance— a debt that could have been paid in a short time. But the forgiven servant wanted his money immediately, so he grabbed the other servant by the throat demanding: "Pay me what you owe" (Matt. 18:28).

"His fellow servant fell down at his feet and begged him, saying, 'Have patience with me, and I will pay you all.'" (Matt. 18:29). But the forgiven servant would not grant his fellow servant's request for time to repay, but cast his fellow servant into prison (Matt. 18:30).

Some other servants told the king what had happened. Then the king confronted the forgiven servant, rebuking him. "You wicked servant! I forgave you all that debt because you begged me. Should you not also have had compassion on your fellow servant, just as I had pity on you?" (Matt. 18:32-33)

Notice carefully: The king said that the forgiven servant had "begged him." The king did not say that the forgiven servant asked to be forgiven— he only begged for more time to repay. There was no way the forgiven servant could have paid his debt.

The king was saying, "Shouldn't you have forgiven your fellow servant just as I forgave you? You didn't ask me to forgive you, you just asked for more time to pay— but I forgave you. Your fellow servant didn't ask to be forgiven, he just asked for more time to repay. Shouldn't you have forgiven him unconditionally, just as I forgave you unconditionally?"

In like manner, believers are **released** from the debt *(penalty)* of each and every sin **unconditionally— even if** they do not confess their sins or ask to be forgiven (1 John 2:1). Because God does this for us, as the parable teaches, we must pray and unconditionally release to God the penalty of each offense against us.

We are to forgive unconditionally, just as we are forgiven unconditionally, time after time and day after day. We are to pray and forgive unconditionally— without the necessity of being asked.

Returning to our text: The king was exceedingly angry and turned the unforgiving servant over to the "torturers" (Matt. 18:34). *(The words "tormentors" or "torturers" are good translations. In contrast, "inquisitors" is too soft a word, unless one thinks of the Spanish Inquisition.)* The teaching is that the king did something that brought the unforgiving servant physical anguish, mental anguish, or both.

Then Jesus makes the application— He applies His illustration to you and me. Referring to the action of the king against the unforgiving servant, Jesus says, "So My heavenly Father also will do to you if each of you, from his heart,[2] does not forgive his brother his trespasses"[3-5] (Matt. 18:35). Or paraphrased, "If you do not forgive whenever offended, God will bring anguish into your life."

The teaching of Jesus is disturbingly clear. Chastisement will come from a loving God if we do not obey Him in forgiveness.

Will this chastisement come from failure to use vertical forgiveness, horizontal forgiveness, or both? While the teaching of Matthew 18:23-35 is vertical forgiveness, logic favors the conclusion that both kinds of forgiveness are included. Any refusal to obey God is a sin.

Further, the fact that Jesus was teaching about horizontal forgiveness in the preceding context is another reason to believe that He was including both kinds of forgiveness in Matthew 18:35.

This chastisement will come from a loving God who wants us to be in fellowship with Him through obedience to His commandments (Matt. 6:15, 18:35; Mark 11:25; Heb. 12:6). Avoiding chastisement is the eleventh reason to use vertical forgiveness.

In summary, in addition to the seven reasons to obey God by using **vertical forgiveness** that were tabulated earlier, there are four additional reasons:

- God has forgiven us.

- He has forgiven us **more**.

- He has forgiven us **unconditionally**.

- Obeying God will avoid His chastisement.

Why use **vertical forgiveness**? Why pray and **unconditionally** forgive? We have considered eleven biblical reasons, but one should be sufficient— God commands it.

Summary

God has made it clear that we must use **vertical forgiveness** whenever we have anything against anyone. That is, we must pray and **unconditionally** forgive the penalty of the offense whenever we hold anything against anyone— even though our offender does not repent or ask to be forgiven (Mark 11:25). One of the most instructive passages on forgiveness is the passsage of Matthew 18:23-35.

In this passage, a servant owed the king a huge debt. It was so large the servant could never have paid it. And yet the king forgave him his debt— even though the servant didn't **even** ask to be forgiven.

Then, when the king heard that the one whom he had forgiven so much had not forgiven his fellow servant a mere pittance, he became angry and punished the unforgiving servant— even though the fellow servant had not asked to be forgiven.

This illustration that Jesus gave, teaches that: in like manner **as** God has released us from the penalty of our sins unconditionally, time after time *(since the moment of our saving faith and justification)* by His repetitive judicial forgiveness, **even so**, when others offend us, we are to unconditionally release to God the penalties of their offenses by the use of vertical forgiveness.

Including the teaching in this illustration of the king and his servants, we have seen eleven biblical reasons to use **vertical forgiveness**— to pray and unconditionally forgive *(release to God)* the penalty of offenses:

- Doing so is obeying a command of God.
- Obeying God in vertical forgiveness is one way to love Him.

- Obeying God in vertical forgiveness maintains fellowship with God.

- Obeying God in vertical forgiveness maintains power in prayer.

- Offenses against you are really against God. *(It is God's right to get even, not ours.)*

- God will judge and punish offenders.

- Jesus died for the sins of those who offend us. *(Justice has been done.)*

- God has forgiven us.

- He has forgiven us more.

- He has forgiven us unconditionally.

- Obeying God will avoid His chastisement.

Why use **vertical forgiveness**? Why should we pray and **unconditionally** release to God the penalties of the offenses of others against us? There are at least eleven biblical reasons, but one reason should be enough— God has commanded it. Will you obey Him?

Chapter Six

I Don't Feel Like It!

You might ask, "What if I don't feel like forgiving? Can I forgive if I don't feel like it? How can I? How must I feel before I will be able to forgive? How will I know that I have forgiven? After I have done what I can to forgive, what if I don't feel that I have forgiven?"

The answer to these questions is where the puzzle and power of forgiveness leave the realm of theory and become personal reality. This is where Christians who understand the puzzle of forgiveness can put the power of forgiveness victoriously into action.

A Feeling or a Fact?

If we look for the basic characteristic of forgiveness, what should we expect to find? Is forgiveness something that I will feel or is it something that I must do? Or could it be that forgiveness is a fact, no matter how I feel?

I had observed Janet *(not her real name)* on several occasions in the insurance office where she worked as a computer operator. She would have been unusually attractive if it had not been for a countenance that revealed a bitter spirit.

Each time I saw her I thought, "She's bitter about something. She may not know the importance of forgiving, the reasons why she must forgive, or how to forgive. Or she may not be willing to forgive. Perhaps some day I will have an opportunity to help her."

A year or so later she came in for counseling, and I learned the reason for her bitterness. She told me about her husband's lying, his adulteries, and his continued contacts with another woman. Dick *(not his real name)* admitted everything, but he insisted that now he was merely keeping in contact with a friend for whom he had no romantic or sexual interest.

I showed Janet that the Scriptures are quite clear in teaching a kind of forgiveness that we call vertical forgiveness— a forgiveness in which the penalty of each offense must be forgiven unconditionally. That is, since all sin is against God and it is His right to judge and to punish, we are commanded to release to Him our supposed right to get even (Mark 11:25; Rom. 12:19). Then, after "handing up" to God the penalty of each offense, our actions toward the offender must be characterized by *agape* love.

Bound Only by *Agape* Love

This is important: after using vertical forgiveness to release to God the penalty of an offense, our actions toward the offender must be governed by our purposeful dedication to the good of the offender— **this is *agape* love.**[1-5] Loving the offender *(the penalty of whose offense we have forgiven by vertical forgiveness)* includes not doing or saying anything that is vengeful— including any kind of gossiping.

However, loving the offender *(the penalty of whose offense we have forgiven by vertical forgiveness)* does not necessarily mean "acting as if we have forgotten the offense." And it does not necessarily mean "never mentioning it again."

Instead, loving the offender *(the penalty of whose offense we have forgiven)* means doing whatever is best for him, whether or not doing those things pleases him. In some instances, "acting as if we have forgotten" is the loving thing to do, and in some not necessarily different situations "never mentioning it again" is the loving thing to do. In other situations, *agape* love demands doing things that are painful, costly, and/or embarrassing to an offender *(whose penalty has been released to God)*.

For example, Mike awakens suddenly in the middle of the night. He hears a scuffling noise and a muffled cry coming from the bedroom of his teenage daughter, Millie. Opening the door to Millie's bedroom, he sees a man attempting to carry Millie out an open window. It is Burt, a highly undesirable fellow whose advances Millie had rejected repeatedly. After an intense fight, Mike subdues Burt, and the police are on their way.

At breakfast, Mike, his wife, and all of his children pray, thanking God for protecting Millie. Mike reminds his family that God commands them to pray and release to God the penalty of every offense against them, including Burt's. As hard as it seems to obey, God's commandment to use vertical forgiveness applies to them. They must pray and turn over to God the penalty of Burt's offense for God's judgment and punishment. After some hesitation, each of them prays and releases to God the penalty of Burt's offense.

Later the police ask Mike to file charges against Burt. But they had all prayed and had unconditionally released to God the penalty of Burt's offense. Now what can they do? What should they do?

Their act of vertical forgiveness was a verbal contract with God in which they relinquished to God that which belongs to God— the right to avenge wrongs. They can take any action that is good for Burt or that is good for society— as long as that action is not taken as an act of vengeance.

Mike can and should file charges against Burt. For the good of the offender, for the good of society, and as an example and warning to others, charges should be filed.

But this is not their entire obligation. Mike's family should pray for Burt daily, especially for his salvation. This is one way they can love Burt with *agape* love (Luke 6:27-28). They should pray that both the trial and Burt's punishment will be for his good and for the good of society (Rom. 13:1-4), that the outcome will be according to God's will, and that it will bring glory to Him.

It would be good for Mike, for other believers, and for Mike's pastor to call on Burt in jail. However, it would not be appropriate for Millie to go. Millie can and should pray for him.

Perhaps there is someone who has offended you deeply. As I talk to you about it you may say, "I don't hate him, resent him, or even dislike him. In fact, I love him. I just don't feel comfortable being around him."

But have you obeyed God's command to use vertical forgiveness? Have you ever prayed and unconditionally released to God the penalty of your offender's offense? Have you **really** turned over to God the penalty of his offense? Or has time merely dulled your feelings?[6] Is it like a wound that has scabbed over but has pockets of infection inside? If you are not absolutely sure that you have prayed and unconditionally forgiven the penalty of his offense, then be sure. Do it now, whether or not you have any bad feelings.

Or it may be that you don't **feel** like forgiving. Many Christians do not understand that obedience to God's command to forgive requires **acts of the will**, not acts motivated by feelings. They have the false idea that they must "feel like forgiving," have an "attitude of forgiveness," or have a "spirit of forgiveness."

Feelings Deny the Fact

Consider this scene. Jack owes you ten dollars. You have come to ask for your money. Jack moans, "Oh, I can't possibly pay you now. I lost my job, the roof is leaking, we have hardly any food in the house, the kids are sick, and an uninsured motorist demolished our car."

You doubt Jack's story. You think to yourself, "The deadbeat! He could pay me if he would."

While this thought is still going through your mind, Jack pleads, "Will you forgive me the ten dollars? It is more than I can bear to owe you this debt on top of all my other troubles."

You think, "I'll probably never get it anyway. I might as well." So, after a period of hesitation, you say with obvious reluctance, "Well, O.K."

As you leave, you are angry with yourself. You think, "Why did I let him trick me into saying that I would forgive him?" But as the days go by, your anger subsides. Then you hear that Jack has a new job, and you think, "I will go back to see him. Perhaps he will pay me now."

So next week you go to Jack. "How about paying me that ten dollars you owe me?"

Jack replies, "I don't owe you anything. You forgave me the ten dollars that I owed you." And so you had.

As illustrated in this imaginary scene, forgiveness is an act of the will. You did not have a "spirit of forgiveness" or an "attitude of forgiveness." You did not want to forgive Jack, but reluctantly and begrudgingly **you did**.

After you had forgiven Jack, you did **not** "feel like" you had. You didn't even want to accept the fact that you had forgiven him, so you tried to collect the forgiven debt. Obviously you had not forgotten about it because the remembrance of it made you angry. But the fact is, you did it— you forgave Jack.

As illustrated in this story, forgiveness is an act, not a feeling. "Good feelings" are not a prerequisite for forgiveness— to unconditionally use vertical forgiveness or to grant horizontal forgiveness to a repentant offender. All that is needed is a volitional decision to obey God.

Confirming the Fact

In addition, good feelings are **not** necessary to confirm the fact that you have really released the penalty of each offense to God. Your feelings toward the offender **may not** change at the time.

What if you have prayed and released the penalty of some offense, and then later you felt anger coming back. Ask yourself, "Did I pray and release to God the penalty of this offense?" If you can say, "Yes, God commands that the penalty of each offense be released to Him, and I did it," then confirm that fact in prayer.

Pray something like this: "Lord, I turned the penalty over to You, because You have told me to, and because You have forgiven me much more. I am trusting You to do whatever should be done about the one who offended me. My feelings toward the one who offended me have not changed, but I have obeyed You— I have released the penalty to You. Please change my feelings toward my offender when You are ready. In the meantime, I will do as you command. I will love him with *agape* love by doing things purposefully for his good no matter how I feel."

Right Motives

But what about motives? Your motive for forgiving the penalty of an offense should not be a selfish attempt to feel good. In like manner, your motive for loving your offender with *agape* love should not be a selfish attempt to feel good. Instead, the motive should be obedience to God. However, in response to obedience, God graciously changes feelings.[7]

Helpless without Vertical Forgiveness

Let's go back to the punch-in-the-nose example. Someone hit you in the nose. There was no warning. You had not offended this person. But suddenly his fist met your nose with a violent force. He laughed to see your surprise and to hear your exclamation of pain.

He is far from being repentant. Now each time you see him, he points at you and laughs. Even if he were a thousand miles away, it would not lessen your resentment. He may die without ever repenting of his act, and if he were dead your feelings would be the same. It is extremely doubtful that he will ever ask you to forgive him.

Releasing to God the penalty of an offense is an act of the will that may be diametrically opposite to the way you feel. If our Lord's command to forgive whenever you have anything against anyone means that you must first have an attitude of forgiveness or a spirit of forgiveness, then you have a problem.

If you don't understand that the vertical forgiveness of Mark 11:25 is unconditional release to God of the penalty of the offense, and that it is entirely different from the horizontal forgiveness *(dependent upon the offender's repentance)* taught in Luke 17:3, then you have a problem indeed.

You are stuck with the fact that this guy hit you in the nose, you didn't like it then, and it makes you angry each time you think about it. His offense still makes you angry, and there is nothing that you can do about it.

Don't Try to Fool Yourself

You might try to solve your problem by trying to rationalize his offense, or to find some way to excuse him. You might say, "If I could just understand why he did it."

I would reply, "It doesn't matter why he did it. Pray and release to God the penalty of his offense. Besides, I know why he did it. It was sin."

Or you might say, "I understand why he did it. He had a bad childhood. His father physically abused him." If you are trying to understand him, it is likely that you are trying to excuse him. Just release to God the penalty of the offense, and let Him determine the extent of the offender's guilt.

Attempting to "understand" offenders won't work. It is like sweeping dirt under the rug. You may try to convince yourself that the room is clean, but the rug is getting lumpy.

You may be telling yourself, "Christians don't have bad feelings toward others, and I am a Christian, so I don't have any bad feelings toward him." Make sure you are not deceiving yourself.

Or you may say, "Of course I have forgiven!"

And I reply, "How do you know that you have? When did you do it? How did you do it? Remember, forgiveness is a fact. If you have done it, you should **know** how and when you did it. If you can't remember your act of forgiving or when you forgave, it is quite likely that you never did."

Or perhaps you say, "I asked God to forgive him." If so, you have missed the whole concept of forgiving the penalty of the offenses of others.[8-9] The direction of vertical forgiveness is **upward**. When you pray and unconditionally forgive, you are releasing to God the penalty of the offense for His judgment of the offender. God commands you to hand up the matter to Him. He does not command you to ask Him to release the offender from the penalty of his sins.

Being Obedient is Not Equivalent to Being a Hypocrite

But you may say, "I don't feel like forgiving. I don't have an attitude of forgiveness. The way I feel, if I forgave the penalty of his offense I would be a hypocrite."

How many people went to work this morning who didn't feel like going? As their alarm clocks sounded, they thought, "Oh, no! Not again today!" But then they reminded themselves that they must feed their families and pay their bills. Are they hypocrites by going to work when they don't feel like going?

Did Jesus want to go to the cross? No! His feelings were screaming, "The physical pain of crucifixion is horrible, and it will be worse for me than for anyone who has ever been crucified. I will suffer for all who ever sinned or who will ever sin" (2 Cor. 5:21; Heb. 12:2; Is. 53). Surely no believer would infer that Jesus was a hypocrite for going to the cross without "feeling like it"!

Are you holding something against someone? Be obedient: use vertical forgiveness— pray and release to God the penalty of the offense. Put the power of vertical forgiveness into action in your life.

Actions or Words That Contradict

How can you know that you have forgiven? Vertical forgiveness is an act of the will— not feelings. If you have, as an act of the will, turned over to God the penalty of an offense, then you have forgiven whether or not your feelings confirm the fact.

But be careful that your forgiveness is factual. Vertical forgiveness is a verbal contract with God in which the offended believer releases to God the penalty of an offense, agreeing with God that it is His business to judge and to punish. This verbal contract can't be made with "fingers crossed." If a believer were to attempt to avenge himself *(even with a prayer request)* after supposedly releasing to God the penalty of the offense, would you say that he had really forgiven?

Your feelings may, or may not, change at the time you pray and release to God the penalty of an offense. It is not likely that you will forget the offense— you cannot forget anything as an act of the will. However, after God has taken away the bad feelings, it will not matter whether or not you remember the offense.

If after using vertical forgiveness you still have bad feelings toward the offender, pray and reconfirm the fact that you have forgiven. And while God is changing your feelings toward the offender, pray for him daily, "Lord, bless him," even if initially you have to grit your teeth.

Summary

You might ask, "What if I don't feel like forgiving? Can I forgive if I don't feel like it? How can I? How must I feel before I will be able to forgive? How will I know that I have forgiven? After I have done what I can to forgive, what if I don't feel that I have forgiven?"

Vertical forgiveness is an **act of the will** *(that may be contrary to feelings)* in which the penalty of an offense is released to God unconditionally. It is not necessary for the offender to repent or for him to ask you for forgiveness *(for you to release to God the penalty of the offense)*. Your offender may be a thousand miles away. He may be dead. And he may never know that you have released the penalty of his offense to God.

Vertical forgiveness is release to God of the penalty of the offense. It is because the penalties of offenses are released upward to God that we call it vertical forgiveness.

It is **not** necessary to have an "attitude of forgiveness" or a "spirit of forgiveness" to release to God the penalties of offenses. You are not a hypocrite for obeying a command of God when you don't "feel like it."

Can you know that you have forgiven? Yes. Vertical forgiveness is a fact, not a feeling. It is the result of an act of the will. **If** you have, as an act of the will, turned over to God the penalty of an offense, **then** you have forgiven.

But be careful that **your** forgiveness is a fact. Vertical forgiveness is a verbal contract with God. If a believer were to attempt to slander an offender after supposedly releasing to God the penalty of the offense, would you say that he had really forgiven?

Your feelings may, or may not, change at the time that you pray and unconditionally forgive. It is **not** likely that you will forget the offense— you **cannot** forget anything as an act of the will. But after God has taken away the bad feelings, it will not matter whether or not you remember the offense.

If after forgiving the penalty of an offense you still have bad feelings toward the offender, pray and reconfirm the fact that you have forgiven.

And **while waiting** for God to change your feelings, pray for the offender daily. Even if initially you have to grit your teeth, pray, "Lord, bless him."

Chapter Seven

Warning! Deep Ditches on Both Sides!

What do you suppose Jesus means when He says "Take heed to yourselves" (Luke 17:3)? Perhaps He is saying, "Warning! Be careful. Some will offend you, and unless you are careful, you are likely to respond to them wrongfully, stumbling and falling into a 'ditch' on one side of the road or the other."

If we are to heed this warning, we must achieve a balanced understanding of the instructions given by our Lord. We must consider not only the immediate context, but also other Scriptures that teach principles for solving problems in interpersonal relationships.

Jesus says, "Rebuke the person who offends you" (Luke 17:3, paraphrased). Why should we rebuke him? It is imperative to understand this point. You are to rebuke the offender for **his good**!

As a believer, are not dependent upon the offender's repentance. You have the power of vertical forgiveness (Mark 11:25). You can deal with offenses by praying and releasing to God the penalty of each offense!

But God insists that the offender get right with you. He is out of fellowship with God unless he tries to get right with you (Matt. 5:23-24). You are to rebuke him to bring him to repentance, with the objective of restoring him to fellowship with both God and yourself. And yet, you are to "take heed" that you do not fall into a "ditch."

Avoid the Deepest Ditches

Janet stumbled and fell into a ditch. Dick had been unfaithful to Janet. Week after week I asked Janet if she had prayed and unconditionally forgiven the penalty of his offenses. She defiantly said, "No!"

In her rebellion against God, she had fallen out of fellowship with Him. She wasn't praying at all; but if she had, it is doubtful that God would have "heard" her prayers (Ps. 66:18). She had fallen into the ditch of allowing an offender to harm her fellowship with God.

After a struggle of several weeks between her emotions and her will, Janet released to God the penalty of Dick's offenses. Later, Dick came to Janet saying that he was sorry and asking her to forgive him. Should she restore him to fellowship with herself by granting him horizontal forgiveness?

One deep ditch to avoid is allowing the offenses of others to keep you out of fellowship with God by your refusal to use vertical forgiveness when offended. Another deep ditch is refusing to obey God's command to grant horizontal forgiveness to every repentant offender. But there are more ditches to avoid.

Don't Take the "Easy Way"

Perhaps you are thinking, "Confrontation can result in an unpleasant, even nasty, dispute. It is easier to use vertical forgiveness *(releasing to God through prayer the penalty of the offense)* and go my way." Certainly it is easier. Remember, Jesus says, "Take heed to yourselves." One ditch to avoid is the selfish tendency to sidestep unpleasant duties.

93

Chapter Seven-----Warning! Deep Ditches on Both Sides!

Don't Gossip

The circle of knowledge should be kept as **small** as possible (Matt. 18:15-17). It should include only those who are a part of the problem or a part of the solution to the problem. This principle precludes such sinful and harmful practices as gossip and "juicy" prayer requests.

Don't Use Corrupt Words

Take heed to yourself. Your words are to **edify** *(build up)* the offender, not tear him down with corrupt words (Eph. 4:29).

If you do not use vertical forgiveness, praying and releasing to God the penalty of the offense, **before** confronting the offender, there is danger that your words may be "corrupt," hurtful, and harmful.

Don't Judge from Past Failures

Jesus had said, "If your brother sins against you, rebuke him; and if he repents, forgive him" (Luke 17:3). One of His disciples may have been asking himself, "How can I be sure that my brother is really repentant?"

You may be asking yourself, "The one who offended me may do it again. How can I know that he is sincere? How long should I observe his behavior to see if he has really repented? If I forgive him too hastily, he may hurt me again. I don't want to be a doormat."

Perhaps Jesus continued his teaching in the next verse to answer questions such as these. Jesus said, "And if he sins against you seven times in a day, and seven times in a day returns to you, saying, 'I repent,' you shall forgive him" (Luke 17:4).

Jesus' astonished disciples responded, "Increase our faith." Their astonishment might be more fully

expressed with an old slang word— they were flabber-
gasted. They wondered, "How could we possibly grant
forgiveness to someone who has proven himself to be
so insincere?" They concluded that it would be possible
only if their faith were increased.

After briefly teaching about faith, Jesus continued
his teaching about horizontal forgiveness.[1] He told about
a servant who had done as he was commanded by his
master, even though the master's treatment of the servant
seemed severe (Luke 17:7-9). Then, in Luke 17:10, Jesus
applied His story to the spiritual realm. He said, "So
likewise you, when you have done all those things which
you are commanded, say, 'We are unprofitable servants.
We have done what was our duty to do.'"

What was Jesus saying? "You are not your own . . .
you were bought at a price . . ." (1 Cor. 6:19-20). "But
why do you call Me 'Lord, Lord,' and not do the things
which I say?" (Luke 6:46). "If you love Me, keep My
commandments" (John 14:15).

Jesus had presented a "what if" situation: "If he sins
against you seven times and seven times in the same day
returns and repents, *(then)* you shall forgive him. You
cannot refuse to grant horizontal forgiveness on the basis
of past performance." (Luke 17:4, paraphrased). That is
one of the reasons that Jesus says, "Be careful" (Luke
17:3, paraphrased).

Don't Demand Proof

Luke 17:4 shouts loudly that the offender's **past**
failures **cannot** be used as a basis for refusing to grant
horizontal forgiveness. Just as insistently, this verse
demands that the offended person **must not** make the
offender prove, by his performance over a period of
time, that he is really repentant.

95

Chapter Seven-----Warning! Deep Ditches on Both Sides!

But if we shouldn't judge the offender's alleged repentance on the basis of his past performance, and if we shouldn't withhold granting horizontal forgiveness until the offender can prove that he is really repentant, must we grant horizontal forgiveness on the basis of mere physical movement toward us together with alleged repentance?

In Luke 17:4, the Greek word translated "turn" in some versions *("return" in other versions)* can be used to convey a variety of meanings, from a mere physical turning to a real change of heart *(repentance)*. The question is: Which meaning does it have here?[2-10]

It would be easier to support an argument that "turning" refers to nothing more than physical move-ment— a physical returning for the purpose of saying that he repents. For the sake of argument, let's take the "easier to prove" interpretation. Let's assume that "turn to you" *(or "return to you")* refers to a physical returning of the offender.

If an offender "turns to you" *("returns to you")* saying that he repents, his physical action of returning to you for the purpose of alleging repentance **implies** a supposed repentance, and his words verbally express the same thing. Also notice that in Luke 17:3 the subject is repentance and forgiveness, and then in 17:4 a "what if" situation is presented.

Therefore, to "turn" in Luke 17:4 **must imply** sup-posed repentance because: (1) the physical act of his returning is for the purpose of alleging repentance; (2) in the context, Luke 17:3, the subject is repentance; and (3) the "what if" situation of Luke 17:4 continues the discussion of repentance.

Don't Grant Forgiveness to the Unrepentant

After a period of time, Dick "returned" *(came back)* to Janet, and he alleged repentance. However, in spite of her earnest pleading, he stubbornly refused to quit calling the other woman. Should she grant Dick horizontal forgiveness?

His physical movement toward Janet **implied** a supposed repentance, and his words **alleged** repentance, but his refusal to quit calling the other woman **contradicted** his alleged repentance.

Dick's refusal to quit calling the other woman contradicted both his "turning" and his "saying." To grant horizontal forgiveness in the face of an unrepentant spirit would **not** be the loving thing for Janet to do. She needs to withhold granting of horizontal forgiveness **until** there is an absence of anything that contradicts his alleged repentance.

Don't Relieve God's Pressure

Granting horizontal forgiveness when **present** evidence *(not past performance)* contradicts the offender's alleged repentance **is wrong**. It is unwise. It is wrong because it is not the loving thing to do. Love means doing what is best for the other person. Instead, it may be a selfish attempt to avoid the more difficult path, an unpleasant path, but the loving path that God would have you take.

For the offender to be brought to repentance, he needs to feel the estrangement that his sin has caused, both between himself and God and between himself and you. Don't fall into the ditch of granting horizontal forgiveness when there is **present** evidence that alleged repentance is not genuine.

97

Chapter Seven-----Warning! Deep Ditches on Both Sides!

Don't Forget Restitution

Zacchaeus said to Jesus, "If I have taken anything from anyone by false accusation, I restore fourfold" (Luke 19:8). "Take heed" that your granting of horizontal forgiveness is in the best *(spiritual)* interests of the offender. If an offender is **really** repentant, he will be willing to make restitution.

Loving an offender who has financially defrauded you may include requiring a plan for repayment *(restitution)* before granting horizontal forgiveness. To grant horizontal forgiveness to an offender who is not willing to make restitution may release the pressure that God wants to keep on him so that he will really repent. Determine whether or not restitution is appropriate **before** you grant horizontal forgiveness.

Don't Let Feelings Stop You

Finally, Dick told Janet that he had terminated all communication with the other woman. How could Janet believe him? He had proven to her that he was a liar.

At that time almost a thousand miles separated them from the other woman. But how could Janet be sure that the other woman wouldn't make a trip to see Dick? How could she be sure that he would not become involved with another woman within a few months? What would he have to do, and for how long, for her to be sure that he was really repentant?

Did his supposed turning, along with his alleged repentance, make him eligible for horizontal forgiveness? Yes, in the **absence** of anything that contradicts his supposed repentance *(any current evidence, not past performance)*, she should, she must, grant him horizontal forgiveness.

If at some later date he should be unfaithful again, she must pray and unconditionally release to God the penalty of the new offense. Then, if he came back in supposed repentance and asked to be forgiven again, she must grant him horizontal forgiveness again, unless his **current** *(not past)* behavior contradicted his words.

Perhaps you are out there hurting, and you think that I am being cruel. I am not saying it is always easy to pray and unconditionally forgive, nor am I saying that it is always easy to grant horizontal forgiveness. Instead of being easy, it may be an extremely difficult task for you. It was for Janet. And yet the path of blessing is in obeying God.

Make the Biblical Choice

Will you choose fellowship with God through obedience— unconditionally releasing to God the penalty of each offense by vertical forgiveness, and then granting horizontal forgiveness when your offender repents?

There are well-meaning friends who will say, "Don't let him do that to you. Don't be a doormat." If you obey God, and the other person defies God, who is the winner, you, or the one who is defying God?

Don't Let Feelings Fool You

Whether it be unconditionally releasing to God the penalty of an offense through vertical forgiveness or granting horizontal forgiveness to a repentant offender, the one who forgives should not be bound by any erroneous definition of forgiveness.

For instance, **no one**, not even a believer who has obeyed God in both vertical forgiveness and horizontal forgiveness, **can forget** anything as an act of the will. No one should even try. Unfortunately, many believers

99

Chapter Seven·····Warning! Deep Ditches on Both Sides!

erroneously think that forgiving magically results in a dramatic change of feelings or a lapse of memory. Then when feelings of anger come back, they erroneously think that they haven't forgiven, and some even come to the erroneous conclusion that it is impossible for them to forgive.

Don't Be Confused by Wrong Definitions

Don't be confused by any erroneous definitions of forgiving, such as: "Forgiving is acting as if you have forgotten" or "Forgiving is never mentioning it again." The offended person does **not** have to act as if he has forgotten— **unless** *agape* love[11] demands it. And he can mention it again, **if** it is good for the offender— **if** it is an act of love, not an act of vengeance.

He can say anything to the offender, to the local church,[12] or to civil authorities that is in accordance with the Scriptures and that is good for the offender (Matt. 18:15-17; Eph. 4:15; 4:29). But "take heed to yourselves." Whatever you do must be done in love. Your objective must be the good of the offender.

Do these same things apply to Dick and Janet? Could she take their marriage problem to the church? We will consider this problem in the next chapter.

What will be accomplished when Janet grants horizontal forgiveness? Obviously, something is lacking in their marriage until Dick "gets right" with Janet. He will, or should, feel an "out-of-fellowship" condition both with God and with Janet until he gets right with Janet and with the Lord.

For this reason, horizontal forgiveness can be called "get-right forgiveness." When the offender comes back, saying he repents, he is *(or should be)* doing what he can to get right with the one he has offended.

God says it is so important for the offender to get right with the one he has offended that the offender should not even attempt to worship God until he has tried to be reconciled with the one he has offended (Matt. 5:23-24). This is logical. How can a believer really come before God to worship Him unless he has obeyed God by doing what he can to right his wrong?

Remember Basic Principles

Going back to basics: believers have the power of vertical forgiveness— praying and releasing to God the penalty of each offense against them. Thus, believers who understand vertical forgiveness and practice it are not dependent upon the repentance of their offenders. To these believers, as God intends it to be, horizontal forgiveness is for the good of the offender.

However, the offender can use the good of horizontal forgiveness to help the one he has offended. Let's consider some ways he can help.

If the offended person is a believer, he may not have been willing to obey God by unconditionally forgiving the penalty of the offense, thus keeping himself out of fellowship with God. If the offender comes in repentance, asking for forgiveness, the offended person may then be willing to obey God in horizontal forgiveness. In addition, many believers do not know that they can pray and unconditionally forgive the penalty of each offense. They need help.

Or if the offender is a believer and the person he has offended is an unbeliever, the offense of the believer may be a stumbling block. The offending believer may be standing in the way of the offended person's decision to become a believer.

101

Chapter Seven-----Warning! Deep Ditches on Both Sides!

In trying to get right with the one he has offended, a believer may help the other person spiritually and/or emotionally. At least he has the satisfaction of being obedient to a commandment of God, and of doing what he can to get right with the one he has offended.

Sexual Relations After Adultery

Left unanswered thus far is a question that, most likely, many readers have had in their minds, "What about sexual relations after adultery?" Must Janet resume sexual relations with Dick? Before he repents, or after? When? Under what conditions?

These are important questions to address, especially with the increase in occurrence, variety, and severity of sexually transmitted diseases. This subject is addressed in Appendix C.

Know What You Are Granting

Let's take the illustration of Mike, Millie, and Burt a step further. Prior to the trial, Burt sent word to the family that he wanted to see them. He told them that he had accepted Jesus Christ as his Savior. With tears in his eyes, Burt told them how remorseful he was and asked them to forgive him for attempting to abduct Millie.

After Burt finished speaking, Mike said, "In asking for forgiveness, are you trying to remove the barriers between us so that you can have fellowship with us in the future? Or are you asking that we not testify against you, help you get a reduced sentence, or get you released from the penalty of your crime? We need to know what you are asking, and what we would be granting."

Burt replied, "I . . . well . . . I . . . I guess in all of those ways."

Mike responded, "All sin is against God. It is His right to punish sin even though we may feel or even erroneously think that we have a right to get even. So, in obedience to God, we have prayed and released to God the penalty of your offense.

"But you say that you are a Christian now. God cannot punish believers for their sins. The penalty for believers' sins has been paid on the cross. He chastens believers who sin, for their good. Often there are terrible temporal consequences of sin, and there can be loss of eternal rewards, but God does not punish believers for their sins.[13]

"Having prayed and turned over to God the penalty of your offense, we cannot treat you badly. Instead, we must do those things that we believe are good for you.

"One way we can do good for you is by praying for you, and every day since you tried to abduct Millie, we have prayed that God would bring you to Himself in salvation, and that He would use whatever punishment you may get for your good and for His glory.

"As taught in Romans 13:1-4, God has ordained civil governments as His servants to provide order and safety in society and to punish evildoers. It would be wrong for us to interfere with the God-ordained function of civil government by attempting to have you freed, or even by attempting to have your sentence reduced. God is sovereign in the affairs of men. Whether your judge is a believer or an unbeliever, his verdict will be the one that God can use for your good— to conform you to the likeness of Jesus, as revealed in Romans 8:28-29.

"It is our duty to cooperate with God-given functions of civil government. Because of this we must testify against you, honestly, but without rancor. We want God's good for you.

103

Chapter Seven·····Warning! Deep Ditches on Both Sides!

"As to your future fellowship with my family, God must lead in this. We know from John 20:2 that Jesus had special friends. It is not wrong for some Christians to have closer fellowship with some believers than with others. If you should become a member of our local church, my family will not snub you, but we may never become the best of friends, and Millie may never value you as a friend.

"There is also a problem of trust. Trust must be earned. It is foolish to trust those who have recently shown themselves to be untrustworthy. Even though sinners saved by grace are perfectly acceptable to God, they are not necessarily eligible for positions of trust. First Samuel 16:7 teaches that God sees the heart, but man sees only outward appearances. Would you put a recently convicted criminal on the police force, even if he now professed salvation?

"So, Burt, if you are trying to get right with us for what you did, we will be obedient to God and grant horizontal forgiveness to you now, even as we were obedient and released to God the penalty of your offense by vertical forgiveness. Is that what you want?"

Burt replies, "Yes, I do want to get right with you as much as I can. I really wanted all of those other things too, but the important thing is that I obey my Savior. Will you forgive me?"

"Yes, Burt, I forgive you," Mike responds, and one by one the others tell Burt that they forgive him.

The Effects of Horizontal Forgiveness

Granting horizontal forgiveness does not necessarily establish relationships that had not previously existed. If a complete stranger stole my car, then returned it and asked for my forgiveness, I should not feel obligated or compelled to make him my friend. Instead, I would be acknowledging and accepting his attempt to get right with me for his offense.

Those granting horizontal forgiveness need to act prudently and wisely. It would be foolish for Millie to go alone to take a cake to Burt's apartment. She should leave to others acts of friendship and maintain a quiet reserve in any chance encounters with Burt.

She can love Burt with *agape* love by praying for him— without tempting him to see more in her friend-liness than *agape* love for another person for whom Christ died. If Burt really is saved, God will provide those who can minister to his needs— especially as Millie and the other members of her family pray for him.

Putting It All Together

In summary, vertical forgiveness is a volitional act in which an offended believer, in obedience to God, through prayer, releases to God the penalty of an offense even though the offender may be unrepentant— even though the offender may be exulting in his offense. After unconditionally forgiving the penalty of an offense, the offended person can do anything and say anything that is in accordance with *agape* love.

Vertical forgiveness is for the good of the offended. It releases the offended person from bad feelings (Eph. 4:31-32). In contrast, horizontal forgiveness is primarily for the good of the offender.

Horizontal forgiveness is a contract in which the offender declares that he is repentant and specifies what he wants released. The offended person **must** do what-ever he believes to be best for the offender. He **may** *(but is not required to)* release the offender from any debt, such as a sum of money. He **may** grant all or part of the

105

Chapter Seven-----Warning! Deep Ditches on Both Sides!

offender's request, but he **must** grant forgiveness in the sense of releasing the offender from alienation caused by the offense **unless** present circumstances, such as refusal to make restitution, deny the reality of repentance.

Avoid All of the Ditches

Before you confront the offender, be sure that you are spiritually and emotionally ready for a confrontation. Be sure that you are prepared to use words that edify rather than harsh words that wound and destroy. Pray and release to God the penalty of the offense **before** you attempt to confront the one who has offended you.

"Take heed to yourselves." Don't fall into the ditch of easy forgiveness: **rebuke** when it is good for the offender; **require** restitution when it is good for the offender; and **refuse** to grant horizontal forgiveness when there is present evidence that repentance is not genuine.

At the same time, avoid the ditch on the other side of the road: be sure that you **graciously grant** horizontal forgiveness when it is right to do so.

———

Summary

Vertical forgiveness is for the good of the one who has been offended— it **releases him** from pain, anger, or resentment caused by the offense. Vertical forgiveness is God-given power that enables the believer to free himself from the offense of the offender.

In contrast, horizontal forgiveness is primarily for the good of the offender. It helps him as he obeys God, doing what he can to get right with the one he has offended. It helps **release** the **offender** from the burden of his offense as he tries to get right with both God and man.

How often must we grant horizontal forgiveness to an offender? Jesus says, "And if he trespasses against you seven times in a day, and seven times in a day turns again to you, saying, 'I repent,' you shall forgive him" (Luke 17:4, compare KJV).

How believable must supposed repentance be? Since God intends horizontal forgiveness to be used for the good of the offender, it should be granted **unless** there is present evidence *(not past performance)* that the offender has not "turned" from his offensive behavior. Horizontal forgiveness **must not** be withheld because of repeated offenses, and it **must not** be withheld until the offender can prove that he is sincere.

Horizontal forgiveness should be withheld when there is **refusal** to change sinful behavior, or **refusal** to make restitution, because either of these refusals contradicts both the repentance that is implied in a physical returning to you and a verbal expression of repentance.

Granting horizontal forgiveness is so important that Jesus introduced the subject by cautioning, "Take heed to yourselves." If we take His words in context with

107

Chapter Seven·····Warning! Deep Ditches on Both Sides!

other Scriptures, Jesus was saying, "Be careful! Unless you are careful, you will stumble and fall into a ditch." Don't fall into a ditch by:

- Selfishly avoiding confrontation when a rebuke would be good for the offender

- Increasing the circle of knowledge beyond that which is absolutely necessary

- Using "corrupt" words that harm, rather than words that build up

- Withholding horizontal forgiveness on the basis of past performance

- Withholding horizontal forgiveness until such time as the offender can prove his repentance

- Granting horizontal forgiveness when there is present evidence of an unrepentant spirit, such as refusal to make restitution

- Confronting when no confrontation is appropriate and only vertical forgiveness is needed

If you have been offended, **love** your offender by ministering to him through confrontation and horizontal forgiveness. **If** you have been the offender, **minister** to the one you have offended by asking him for horizontal forgiveness.

If you have been the offender, asking the one you offended for horizontal forgiveness may remove a stumbling block that your offense has placed between him and God. If he is an unbeliever, you may remove a stumbling block that is in the way of his salvation. If he is a believer, he may not know about vertical forgiveness, or he may not be willing to use it. Your request for horizontal forgiveness may help him to walk closer to his Lord.

Granting horizontal forgiveness may or may not release the offender from repaying money owed or from making restitution. The offended person may release the offender from the duty to repay, or he may take action through the church to obtain repayment. The guiding rule is that the offended believer must do whatever is the loving thing for the offender.

Granting horizontal forgiveness sometimes restores fellowship to the level prior to the offense. Sometimes it does not. Further, granting horizontal forgiveness does not automatically create a relationship that did not exist prior to the offense— the forgiven person will not necessarily become a friend— but you must love him with *agape* love.

With regard to both vertical forgiveness of the penalty of each offense and horizontal forgiveness of the offender, it is not necessary to act as if it has been forgotten, as some erroneously teach.

Instead the offended person can say anything to the offender, to the church, to civil authorities, or to any other appropriate person that is in accordance with the Scriptures and good for the offender. And he can do anything that is good for the offender.

"Take heed to yourselves." Don't fall into the ditch of easy forgiveness: **rebuke** when it is good for the offender; **require** restitution when it is good for the offender; and **refuse** to grant horizontal forgiveness when there is present evidence that repentance is not genuine.

And avoid the ditch on the other side of the road: be sure that you **graciously grant** horizontal forgiveness when it is right to do so.

Chapter Eight

Love: Tough or Tender?

We hear much about tough love. Should love be tough? Must love be tough to be effective? In what ways should it be tough? Or should love be tender? But can love that is tender be effective? How can we decide whether love should be tough or tender until we define love?

What is love? The Scriptures speak of two kinds—*philia* and *agape*.[1] *Philia* love is a feeling, whether godly or sinfully selfish, and *agape* love is an act of the will—a dedication to someone or something.

Agape is the kind of love described in the portion of the Scriptures known as "the love chapter" (1 Cor. 13). In this passage, *agape* is used in the same sense as John 3:16 which speaks of God loving sinful mankind enough to give His only Son. Both Scripture passages reflect a selfless love.

But the Scriptures also used *agape* in a sinful sense. In a single Bible verse *agape* is used once in a godly sense and twice in a sinful sense. "Do not love *[agape]* the world or the things in the world. If anyone loves *[agape]* the world, the love *[agape]* of the Father is not in him" (1 John 2:15).

Or paraphrased, 1 John 2:15 says, "Do not dedicate yourself to the world's system or to the things that glitter in the world. If anyone dedicates himself to the sinful world system, the love of the Father is not in him."

In contrast with the two sinful uses of *agape* that are in 1 John 2:1, most of the uses of *agape* in the New Testament are in a good sense. How do we know? Because *agape* is used most often of God's love and of love that He commands.

It is helpful to have a definition for *agape* love that reflects how God expects us to love others. First, a rather formal definition is:

> *Agape* love is an act of the will to purpose and to do that which is best for the other person without the necessity of emotional motivation *(feeling like it)*.

Perhaps a more down-to-earth definition would be helpful:

> *Agape* love is an act of the will to purpose and to do whatever is best for the other person—no matter how that person has treated us— even if we have bad feelings toward the one that God commands us to love.

God Says Love Must Be Gentle

Whether our love should be tough or tender depends upon the answer to two questions: "Which kind of love *(agape* or *philia)* is in view?" and "Does God want our love to be tough or tender?" The answer to the first question is obvious— God expects our love for others to be a selfless love that is like His *agape* love for us.

As for the second question, consider these Scriptures:

> Brethren, if a man is overtaken in any trespass, you who are spiritual restore such a one in a spirit of

gentleness, considering yourself lest you also be tempted (Gal. 6:1).

And a servant of the Lord must not quarrel but be **gentle** to all, able to teach, patient, in humility correcting those who are in opposition, if God perhaps will grant them repentance, so that they may know the truth (2 Tim. 2:24-25).

Remind them to be subject to rulers and authorities, to obey, to be ready for every good work, to speak evil of no one, to be peaceable, **gentle**, showing all humility to all men (Titus 3:1-2).

But we were **gentle** among you, just as a nursing mother cherishes her own children (1 Thess. 2:7).

As taught in these four Scripture passages, our love for others should be *agape* love and it should be tender *(gentle)*. But is it possible for love to be both tender and tough? Should our love be both tough and tender?

God Says Love Must Be Tough

God commands that our love be tough enough to speak the truth in *agape* love (Eph. 4:15). Speaking the truth in *agape* love means saying what is best for the other person. Speaking the truth in *agape* love when rebuking an offender may, and hopefully will, make the offender sorrowful— a sorrow that leads to repentance (Luke 17:3; 2 Cor. 7:9).

Agape love must be tough enough to confront when it is good for the offender. And it must be gentle in the act of confrontation. The offender must see gentleness, humility, and a reconciling spirit in the confronter. He must see confrontation as an act of love, not a vengeful act.

Don't Release the Pressure

In earlier chapters of our story about fictitious characters Mike, Millie, and Burt, Burt had tried to abduct Mike's daughter, Millie. Later, while in jail awaiting trial, Burt had become a Christian. At least that is what he said. Then in the last chapter, Burt had sent word to Mike's family that he wanted to talk to them. With a spirit that evidenced repentance, he asked their forgiveness for attempting to abduct Millie. In response, they granted horizontal forgiveness.

But let's change the circumstances and use this story to consider another point about forgiveness. Assume that Burt had **not** repented. What should they do? They had reacted biblically. Using vertical forgiveness they had prayed and unconditionally released to God the penalty of Burt's offense (Mark 11:25). Should they tell Burt that they have forgiven him?[2]

You may have read stories in which someone told an unrepentant offender that he has forgiven him. When viewed superficially, it seems to be the spiritual thing to do. But is it the biblical thing to do? If it is not biblical, it is not right.

Vertical forgiveness is an act of the will in which the **penalty** of an offense, **not the offender**, is unconditionally released to God. After releasing to God the penalty of the offense, the offender remains unforgiven until the one he offended says, "I forgive you."

God says that offenders are to be forgiven when they repent, not before (Luke 17:3). So it is wrong to grant horizontal forgiveness to an unrepentant offender, and it is likewise wrong to tell an unrepentant offender that he has been forgiven.

Consider this: God commands the offender to go to the one he has offended to get right with him (Matt. 5:23-24). In these same verses, God says that this act is so important that it should be done before attempting to worship God. This means that the offender is out of fellowship with God unless he is willing to obey God by trying to get right with the one he has offended.

Is it right to do or say anything that dissuades a believer from taking steps to get right with those he has offended? Obviously it is **wrong**.

But you may be thinking, "Burt was not a believer when Mike and Millie prayed and forgave the penalty of his offense. What about telling an unrepentant offender who is an unbeliever that you have forgiven him?"

First of all, as pointed out above, according to the Word of God the offender is **not** forgiven. Instead, the penalty of the offense has been turned over to God. However, there is another reason that an unsaved offender should not be told that he has been forgiven— an important reason.

Jesus says, "Those who are well have no need of a physician, but those who are sick. . . . I did not come to call the righteous, but sinners, to repentance" (Matt. 9:12-13). Or paraphrased, "I did not come to call those who think they are O.K. I did not come to save those who are satisfied with themselves as they are. Instead, I came to save those who know they are sinners."

Should a Christian seek to lessen the burden of guilt that God may be using to bring a sinner to salvation? No. In spite of sentimental stories that you may have heard, it is **wrong** to tell an unrepentant unbeliever that you have forgiven him.

Instead, a believer can show loving concern for the eternal destiny of the offender. If an opportunity develops, he can make a clear presentation of the Gospel either in person or by mail. In this way he can demonstrate the love of Christ.

One Hundred Percent Responsible

Let's consider God's plans for handling problems between individuals. He has made both the offender and the offended one hundred percent responsible for attempting to achieve restoration to fellowship (Matt. 5:22-23; 18:15-16; Luke 17:3).

God has placed on the offender the responsibility of repenting and asking for forgiveness, but He has also placed on the offended person the responsibility of confronting and rebuking the offender with the goal of bringing him to repentance.

As we consider it, we see that God's procedure for the offended to confront the offender for the offender's good is much like God's love for us. Just as God initiates reconciliation with sinners who caused His Son's death on the cross, it is Christlike for the one who has been offended to help the one who has inflicted injury on him.

When an offender who is a believer gets right with the one he has offended, he is obeying God. God wants the offender's conscience to bring him to repentance. For the offended believer to rebuke him and lead him to repentance is a Christlike act of love. It is an act of love in which the offended helps relieve the offender of the burden of his offense, bringing him back to fellowship with God and with the one he has offended.

Or if the offender is an unbeliever, the offended believer, after handling the problem between God and himself with vertical forgiveness, is ready to present

the Gospel to the offender, thereby attempting to bring
the offender to eternal salvation. What a Christlike thing
for the offended believer to do— to attempt to snatch
from an eternal hell one who has offended him!

Don't Rob an Offender

Telling an unrepentant Christian that you forgive
him may **rob** him spiritually. It may release him from
the pressure of guilt feelings, thereby depriving him of
his duty, his right, and his privilege of getting right with
you. Telling an unrepentant unbeliever that you have
forgiven him may **rob** him of the pressure that God
wants to use to bring the offender to Himself.

Vertical forgiveness of the penalty of the offense of
another releases the offended believer from angry or hurt
feelings the offense caused. But the offender should find
release from the burden of his offense **only when** he
repents and asks for forgiveness from the one whom he
offended, confesses his sin to God, **and** makes restitution, if making restitution is possible or appropriate.

In summary, God wants to use feelings of guilt as
a motivating factor for the offender, whether believer
or unbeliever, to repent. Obviously then it is **wrong** to
short-circuit God's plan— telling the offender that he
is forgiven when, indeed, he is not, thereby relieving
the offender's feelings of guilt before he has reacted
biblically to his guilt feelings.

Confrontation is often a difficult and disagreeable
task. We have the tendency to side-step difficult and
disagreeable tasks. It is tempting to tell an offender, "I
forgive you" or "I have forgiven you," thereby avoiding
the task of confronting him. Avoiding confrontation may
be the easier path, but often it is a sinfully selfish way
of avoiding a God-given responsibility.

Be Careful

Love will say, "As I understand the situation, you did thus and so. If this is really what you did, you offended me and sinned against God in the way you treated me."

Confrontation should **not** be undertaken **until** the injured person has used vertical forgiveness. Instead of trying to conjure up a spirit of forgiveness, the injured person should pray and unconditionally release to God the penalty of the offense, thereby letting God put away his bad feelings toward the offender (Eph. 4:31-32).

The danger of premature confrontation— confrontation before releasing to God the penalty of the offense— is that the offended person may show a vengeful spirit or use unwholesome words (Eph. 4:29). In contrast, God teaches that our words should be appropriate for the need of the other person and should be used for the good of the other person (Eph. 4:29).

Confronting should not be undertaken **until** God has put away most of the bitterness, wrath, and anger. God takes away these feelings after the offended has prayed and has unconditionally released to God the penalty of the offense, though some time may elapse before God changes the feelings (Eph. 4:31-32).

Confirming Vertical Forgiveness

While waiting for God to take away his hurt, anger, or animosity, the offended believer should pray, reconfirming unconditional forgiveness. He can pray, "Lord, you have commanded me to pray and unconditionally release the penalty of his offense to You— and I did. My feelings haven't changed, but my feelings do not alter the fact that I did forgive. Please change my feelings when You are ready.

Loving Your "Enemy"

While waiting for God to change his feelings, the offended believer should love the offender with *agape* love by praying for him daily. Even if the offended person feels as if the offender is an enemy, he should pray for the one who has "spitefully used" him. And as appropriate, he should do good things for him, say good things about him, and compliment him (Luke 6:27-28).

Procedures for Confronting

Not only has God commanded the offended person to attempt reconciliation with the offender by confronting him, but God has also provided a procedure for confrontation (Matt. 18:15-17). Every believer, and every local church, should be familiar with this procedure and be willing to follow it when problems arise.

God has given this procedure for handling problems between believers. The discussion that follows pertains to problems between believers— and the responsibilities of the local church. *(Some of the principles and procedures are also applicable to those who are not believers)*.

Following God's procedure may involve taking only a single step, or it may include taking two, or even three steps— each succeeding step bringing more people into the confrontation.

Not Every Time for Everything

Before considering these three steps, we should look again at the question, "Why confront?" If every Christian went to everyone who annoyed him, at every supposed offense, and at every supposed slight, "much ado" would be made of very little.

Instead of unnecessarily confronting, *agape* love should **cover** a multitude of offenses (1 Pet. 4:8). Any believer can handle a problem between himself and another believer by going to God alone. He should take care of most offenses against himself by praying and unconditionally releasing to God the penalties of the offenses.

Believers do **not** need to confront everyone about everything that offends or irritates them. The offended believer shouldn't go to confront a supposed offender every time he feels slighted. He does **not** need to go— **unless** it is good for the supposed offender.

At the same time, every believer should be alert to see if that supposed slight might be a reflection of a problem between himself and the other person— a problem that would require confrontation for the good of the supposed offender.

For example, if a friend seems to avoid you once, it may be that he had something on his mind, and did not see you. But if he seems to avoid you twice, there may be a problem between you. You may need to confront him.

Minister to the Offender

If you go, go gently, seeking to find out if there is a problem between you. A good way to start is to ask, "I've been wondering, have I offended you in any way?" Perhaps he is holding something— real, imagined, or misunderstood— against you. Perhaps in his eyes, **you** are the offender. Again, if and when you go, it should be for **his** good, not yours.

A supposed offense may be merely a misunderstanding, but it may also be an opportunity to minister to the offended person by asking him to forgive you.

In addition, you may be able both to minister to him and to bring glory to God by making biblical changes in your life and/or making restitution.

The First Step—Go Alone

In the first step toward reconciliation with an offender, God says, "If your brother sins against you, go and tell him his fault between you and him alone . . ." (Matt. 18:15). How much more honorable to go to the other person to confront him for his good, rather than damage his reputation by gossip in a sinful attempt to justify or avenge yourself!

"Between you and him alone"— this is God's plan, keeping the circle of knowledge to a **minimum**. If there is some situation in which you cannot keep the circle to the minimum taught in the Scriptures— or some situation in which you cannot confront him without harming him— be careful. It is quite likely that you should handle the problem between yourself and God by vertical forgiveness, and leave it to God to rebuke the offender through his conscience.

Keeping the circle of knowledge to a minimum rules out not only gossip but also prayer requests that are embarrassingly revealing. Keeping the circle of knowledge to a minimum also rules out both support groups and group therapy if the group interaction includes violating God's instruction of "between you and him alone."

However, the principle of "between you and him alone" is not violated when it would be potentially dangerous to go alone, either physically or morally, or if going alone could be viewed as impropriety. Use wisdom in this.

Further, talking to a pastor or biblical counselor in confidence about a problem should not violate this principle. Your pastor or biblical counselor should counsel you in ways to handle the problem biblically. He should help you handle the problem between you and God, should caution you to keep the circle of knowledge to a minimum, and should help you to determine whether and how you can help the offender.

The Second Step—One or Two Others

If the step of "going alone" fails, the second step should be taken. In this second step, God instructs the offended person to take one or two others with him (Matt. 18:16). Again the circle of knowledge is to be kept to a minimum. The objective remains the same —to help the offender by bringing him to repentance, restoring him to fellowship with God, and restoring him to fellowship with the one he has offended.

Preferably the one or two you take with you should include the pastor, an elder, or a deacon, depending on the type of church government of your *(or his)* local church. Then if this second step should fail, the circle of knowledge will already include at least one person who should be involved in taking the third step.

The Third Step—Church Discipline

Church discipline is the third step (Matt. 18:17). God intends church discipline to be an act of love. This love requires toughness that will not sinfully avoid difficult and probably disagreeable tasks. But it also requires love that is tender— love that seeks to heal, not wound. Its goal is to restore the erring believer to fellowship with God, with the one he has offended, and with the local church.

In the Church, Not in Civil Courts

God's steps for confrontation, including the step of church discipline, are to be used by believers instead of going to the civil courts. Inspired by the Holy Spirit, the Apostle Paul says, "Dare any of you, having a matter against another, go to law before the unrighteous, and not before the saints?" (1 Cor. 6:1). Dare any of you husbands or wives take your marriage problems to a civil court?

"Dare any of you?" This is strong language. Paul justifies this strong language. He says, "Do you not know that the saints will judge the world? And if the world will be judged by you, are you unworthy to judge the smallest matters? Do you not know that we shall judge angels? How much more, things that pertain to this life?" (1 Cor. 6:2-3).

Paul goes on to denounce the use by believers of civil courts to settle disputes: "Now therefore, it is already an utter failure for you that you go to law against one another. Why do you not rather accept wrong? Why do you not rather let yourselves be cheated?" (1 Cor. 6:7).

Why should a believer allow himself to be cheated rather than going to the civil courts? One answer is that God's procedures for confrontation, including church discipline, are acts of *agape* love. Confronting is for the good of the offender by attempting to bring the offender to repentance and to restoration of fellowship with God and the one whom he has offended (1 Cor. 5:1-13, 6:1-5; 2 Cor. 2:4-8; Eph. 4:15).

If the matter cannot be settled and restoration of fellowship achieved by confrontation and/or by church discipline, then taking a matter to the civil courts is obviously more likely to divide than to reconcile. In addition, the name of Christ may be blasphemed by unbelievers as they see believers fighting in the civil courts. A court battle between believers is not a way to bring glory to God (1 Cor. 10:31).

Do It God's Way—Love the Offender

God's steps of confrontation, including church discipline or the threat of church discipline, are for the good of the offender and should be acts of *agape* love. If a threat of church discipline is effective in bringing the erring believer back into fellowship with God and man, then, if there is no compelling reason for others to know, the circle of knowledge should be kept to a minimum. The congregation may never need to know.

The thought comes into the minds of some, "If we use church discipline will it work, or will we drive him farther away from the church?" The decision of whether or not to use church discipline should not be a question of "Will it work?"

The question should be, "What is the biblical and loving thing to do for the individual church member who is stubbornly backsliding? What course of action *(church discipline or an apparent ignoring/approval of sinful behavior)* will provide a good example for youth and adults? Which is most likely to deter the ungodly from blaspheming Christ and His church? Which course of action will bring glory to God?"

What about Marriage Problems?

Do confrontation and church disciple procedures apply to problems in marriage (Matt. 18:15-17)? Is it permissible for a husband to take marriage problems to the church? Is it permissible for a wife, whom God has put under the authority of her husband, to take marriage problems to the church (Eph. 5:22-24)?

If a woman has a husband who professes to be a believer, and if he is not living in accordance with the Word of God, what should she do? It seems reasonable that she start with the gentlest course of action. After all, a mechanic does not use a hammer when a wrench will work.

God has given wives a way to help bring about biblical changes in their husbands. It is the gentlest but the most powerful course of action she can take because it is God's plan. "Wives, likewise, be submissive to your own husbands, that even if some do not obey the word, they, without a word, may be won by the conduct of their wives" (1 Pet. 3:1).

Does this verse refer to husbands who are not saved or to believing husbands who are not walking in obedience to their calling? The Holy Spirit has not made it clear in the Greek New Testament that He is speaking of one category to the exclusion of the other. Therefore, it seems best to understand this verse as one of God's principles for use by wives of both believers and unbelievers.

Whether a husband be a believer or an unbeliever, one of the most powerful ways for a wife to change her husband is to line up with God's plan for marriage. By her biblical submission to her husband— not by teaching, lecturing, or nagging— she is to step out of the way, allowing God free course to bring about biblical changes in her husband.

The same basic principle applies to husbands— do what God says and wait on Him for the results. God says, "Love your wives" (Eph. 5:25). What better way for a husband to help his wife make biblical changes than to dedicate himself, unselfishly, to loving his wife with *agape* love?

It may be that the husband has failed in many ways to love his wife as he should have. Or, he may have had little guilt in their marriage problems. Whichever is the case, and whether or not his wife will accompany him in obtaining biblical counseling, he should seek out a counselor who will focus on what **he** can do to be a better husband, **not** on what his wife has done or failed to do.

Can a wife appeal marriage problems to the church, even if it results in church discipline for her husband? Perhaps— if it is the loving thing to do. However, it is a serious thing to appeal over God-given authority, and such a course should not be undertaken lightly or carelessly. Instead, a wife should examine her attitudes and her behavior to see what changes she should make in her life—and make them—before entertaining the thought of appealing over her husband's authority.

In a surprisingly high percentage of instances, husbands— believers and unbelievers alike— do not object to their wives seeking biblical counseling even if they will not go with their wives, and many will even encourage their wives to obtain counseling. If the counseling that she receives is biblical, the emphasis will be on how the wife should change and how she can handle the problems between herself and her Lord. The focus will be on what **she** can do to be a better wife, **not** on what her husband has done or failed to do.

What could impress her husband more than "a new wife" who consistently and cheerfully does good for him all day long (Prov. 31:12)? And he may be won over by her conduct, even attempting to love her as Christ loved the church (1 Pet. 3:1; Eph. 5:25). It happens!

In counseling, she should learn how to handle problems between herself and her Lord; and she should learn how to make godly changes in her life. When she learns these things, she is likely to decide that an official appeal to the church is unnecessary.

Her love for the Lord and for her husband should cause her to "put a cover over" the affairs of the home, keeping their differences confidential (1 Cor. 13:7 NIV). Then if the husband makes biblical changes in his life, he will not be embarrassed to be a part of the local church. A wife would be unwise to erect a barrier now to their future fellowship and enjoyment in the local church. Likewise, the husband should maintain family confidences.

Yes, husbands or wives can take problems to the church— if their objectives and goals are biblical *(as opposed to being selfish)*— if they follow the principles laid down in Matthew 18:15-17. It is immeasurably better to take a problem to one or two who are in authority in the church, to those who may be able to help and who will keep the circle of knowledge as small as possible, than to gossip about the offending mate. But asking the church to interfere in a marriage should not be the first course of action.

Further, if the church does become involved, whether or not to initiate church discipline should be a decision made by church leaders *(not husband or wife)* and only after "taking one or two with you" proves to be ineffective (Matt. 18:16-17).

Prepare Before There Is a Need

God provides a basic principle for the operation of the church. He says, "Let all things be done decently and in order" (1 Cor. 14:40). This means that the pastor and others having authority in the church, along with all of the members, should know God's procedure for church discipline **before** the need arises.

Practicing church discipline "decently and in order" can minimize the chance of legal action by a disgruntled member and can possibly prevent a large monetary judgment. The church should have pre-established procedures in church discipline that are in accordance with legal considerations. Jesus says, "Be wise as serpents and harmless as doves" (Matt. 10:16).[3]

For Whose Good?

Tough or tender love? If it is biblical, it will be both tough and tender. For whose good? For the good of the offender. In contrast to what is sometimes called "tough love," tough love that is godly "does not seek its own" (1 Cor. 13:5). Biblical love that is both tough and tender is dedicated to the good of the offender. It is dedicated to bringing offending believers to repentance and to fellowship with God and man, and it is dedicated to bringing unsaved offenders to saving faith.

Be careful. Do not confront until you have prepared your heart by praying and unconditionally releasing to God the penalty of the offender's offense. Otherwise, your tough love may not be tender.

Tough and tender love? For the good of the offending believer, yes. For an example in the church and to the world, yes. But even more importantly, to bring glory to God (1 Cor. 10:31; Col. 3:23-24)!

———

Summary

Should love be tough or tender?

If we are to answer this question we need to know what God says about love; and to do this, we need a definition of love. *Agape* love *(the kind of love that God commands)*, is:

> An act of the will to purpose and to do that which is best for the other person without the necessity of emotional motivation *(feeling like it)*.

Perhaps a more down-to-earth definition will be helpful:

> *Agape* love is an act of the will to purpose and to do whatever is best for the other person—no matter how that person has treated us— even if we have bad feelings toward the one that God commands us to love.

Love must therefore be tough enough to do what is best for the offender, even if doing what is best may result in an unpleasant response.

But love must also be tender. When confronted, the offender must see the confrontation as an act of the offended person's desire to please God. He must see it as an act intended for the offender's good and not as a personal attack motivated by vengeance.

As an indispensable aid to making love tender, the offense should be handled **first** by vertical forgiveness *(releasing to God the penalty of the offense)*. Then, **after** God has put away the bitterness, wrath, and anger, the offended person is ready to confront with love that is tender— with words and an attitude that heal.

The purposes for the horizontal forgiveness of Luke 17:3-4 are:

- To release the offender from the burden of his own offense

- To restore him to fellowship with the one he offended

- To restore him to fellowship with God

To motivate the offender to be restored to fellowship with God and man, God has given him a conscience. If his conscience has not been seared, it is a powerful force driving the offender:

- To repent

- To make restitution

- To request forgiveness from the one he has offended

- To confess his sin to God

But if the offender does not seek to be restored to fellowship with God and man, God has laid the responsibility on the offended person— he is to help the offender by following God's procedure of confrontation.

First, the offended person is to go alone; if unsuccessful, he is to take one or two others with him; and then, if still unsuccessful, he is to take the matter to the church. Three steps— all to be taken in *agape* love, all for the good of the offender.

There can be circumstances where going alone is not physically or morally safe, or situations where it may be impossible to keep the circle of knowledge to a minimum or to prevent otherwise harming the offender. Be careful that you help, not harm.

God intends church discipline to be an act of love. This love requires toughness that will not sinfully avoid difficult and probably disagreeable tasks. But it also requires love that is tender— love that seeks to heal, not wound. It has love at its center— love whose goal is to restore the erring believer.

If a threat of church discipline is effective in bringing the erring believer back into fellowship with God and man, the circle of knowledge can be kept small. The congregation may never need to know.

The decision whether to use church discipline should not be a question of "Will it work?" Instead, the questions should be, "What is the loving thing, what will be a good example to others, and what will bring glory to God?"

Do church discipline procedures apply to problems in marriage (Matt. 18:15-17)? Yes, as a last resort. God has given husbands and wives a better way— cooperate with God as he works in your mate's life. Husbands, love your wives, and wives, submit to your husbands (Eph. 5:25; 1 Pet. 3:7).

Love for each other should "put a cover over" the affairs of the home, keeping differences between them confidential (1 Cor. 13:7 NIV). Not only is this the godly thing to do, but also it avoids placing a barrier of embarrassment between the erring marriage partner and future fellowship with the local church.

God's steps for confrontation, including the step of church discipline, are to be used by believers instead of going to the civil courts. Inspired by the Holy Spirit, the Apostle Paul says, "Dare any of you, having a matter against another, go to law before the unrighteous, and not before the saints?" (1 Cor. 6:1). Dare any of you husbands or wives take your marriage problems to a civil court?

Should love be tough or tender? Both. Love should be tough enough to do what is best for the other person. But insomuch as possible, love for others should be gentle.

The objectives of love that is both tough and tender should include: the spiritual good of the offender, and the spiritual good of other believers, both by an example and as a warning.

More importantly, the goals of love that is both tough and tender should be: not only to avoid occasions for the world to blaspheme Christ, but also to selflessly bring glory to God; (1 Cor. 10:31; Col. 3:23-24)!

Chapter Nine

The "Nuts and Bolts" of Horizontal Forgiveness

There were tears in his eyes as Marvin and I stood leaning against his car. I didn't know him very well, but he had just revealed a secret of many years that brought the tears.

I had been sent by our local church to call on Marvin. He had been out of church for twenty years or so. All of that time his wife had taken the children to Sunday school and church, but he would not go. At one time he had been faithful in attendance, but then suddenly he stopped.

I had met Marvin once before, but there had been no opportunity to talk to him personally. But now we were alone, and he told me why he had left the church. He had said or done something to displease one of the leaders in the church. I don't remember what. It was just a clash of personalities.

Who Cares?

Marvin seemed to have the words of this church leader engraved in his mind. Their memory still brought tears to his eyes. He had been told, "We can do just as well without you around here." He had never gone back.

Marvin is not his name, but this is a real story about a real person who had real hurts. He was like many— all too many— who have "fallen through the cracks." They have come to Jesus in saving faith, they have been justified *(at least we have thought so)*, they have seemed to succeed in their Christian walk, and then they are gone. No one knows why. All too often, no one seems to care or even notice that they are gone.

He Should Have Cared

Marvin didn't tell me the name of the church leader who had spoken unkindly to him, and I didn't ask. But I know what happened, and I know what should have happened.

Let's call the offender Lawrence *(not his real name)*. The first night after their exchange of words, Lawrence should have had a problem sleeping. The next day he should have gone to Marvin, admitted his offense, told Marvin how sorry he was, and asked Marvin to forgive him.

In response, Marvin should have said, "Yes, I forgive you." If forgiveness had been asked and granted, Marvin would have been back in church the next Sunday and the two of them could have remained friends.

Who Needs Which Kind?

Perhaps Lawrence did have a problem sleeping. But when morning came, the pressures of the day may have obscured his concern for Marvin. Now it is Sunday, and as he looks across the congregation, he notices Marvin's wife and children, but Marvin is not with them.

What should Lawrence do? Jesus provides the answer when He says, "Therefore if you bring your gift to the altar, and there remember that your brother has

something against you, leave your gift there before
the altar, and go your way. First be reconciled to your
brother, and then come and offer your gift" (Matt.
5:23-24). Lawrence should whisper to his wife, "I need
to find Marvin," and quietly leave the church service.

With so many "Marvins" out in the world who are
hurting, and with so many offenders who should be helping those whom they have offended, this book would not
be complete without including a few "nuts and bolts" of
horizontal forgiveness— the forgiveness that one individual grants to another in response to repentance and a
request for forgiveness.

Further, these nuts and bolts would not be complete
without showing how horizontal forgiveness of the
offender relates to vertical forgiveness *(release to God
the penalty of an offense)*. To do this we need to answer
the following questions:

- Who needs vertical forgiveness?

- Who needs horizontal forgiveness?

- When is horizontal forgiveness needed?

- What does horizontal forgiveness accomplish?

- What basic principles should govern asking for
  and granting forgiveness?

- What relationship, if any, is there between horizontal forgiveness and feelings?

When and by whom is horizontal forgiveness needed? Marvin needed it. Perhaps he yearned for Lawrence
to ask him for forgiveness. But if he had been taught
the biblical principle of vertical forgiveness, he might
not have allowed sinful and callous behavior of another
person to keep him out of fellowship with God and the
local church.

He should have been taught how to use vertical forgiveness— to pray and unconditionally release to God the penalty of Lawrence's offense (Mark 11:25). He also should have been taught that, if it is good for the offender, the offended believer should confront him.

If he had understood both vertical and horizontal forgiveness, he could have used vertical forgiveness to overcome his hurts, and then he could have confronted Lawrence— for Lawrence's good. Unfortunately, as is the situation with all too many "Marvins," he had not been taught these vital truths.

Too many "Marvins" are taught that instead of praying and forgiving the penalty of the offense, they are to *(vainly)* attempt to "feel good" in spite of the wrath, anger, bitterness, or resentment that seem to almost overwhelm them. These "Marvins" are left powerless— powerless until their offenders repent and ask for their forgiveness.

Marvin needed help. Help could have come in one of two ways. First, Lawrence was responsible to help Marvin by expressing his repentance and asking Marvin to forgive him. Or if Lawrence did not have sufficient Christian concern to help Marvin even after he had shoved Marvin into a spiritual ditch, then someone, seeing that Marvin was no longer attending church, should have had sufficient concern to go and pull him out of the ditch.

Someone should have asked Marvin what was wrong. Someone should have taught him about vertical forgiveness *(teaching him to pray and unconditionally forgive the penalty of Lawrence's offense)*, and then should have persuaded him to release to God the penalty of Lawrence's offense. Someone should have taught him— and pleaded with him— for his good.

Why Take A Chance?

Vertical forgiveness should be used by believers for nearly all offenses. But there may be one exception. If an offender should come in repentance, asking to be forgiven, and the offended believer grants horizontal forgiveness *(before the offended believer has prayed and forgiven the penalty of that offense)*, then the offense has been released to the offender, and forgiveness through prayer **may not** be needed.

Why would I say "may not be needed?" Jesus says, "Forgive, if ye *[you]* have ought *[anything]* against any . . ." (Mark 11:25 KJV). If in granting horizontal forgiveness to a repentant offender, an offended believer is convinced that he has released the offender from both the penalty and the alienation caused by the offense, then the use of vertical forgiveness *(to release to God the penalty of the offense)* may not be necessary.

But why should a believer risk being out of fellowship with God? Even though he has said to the offender, "I forgive you," unless he is sure that he has fully met God's requirements, why not pray and tell God that he is turning over to Him the penalty of the offense?

Why not be sure? "Lord, I have granted him forgiveness, releasing him from both the penalty of his offense and the alienation that it caused between us. I think that in granting horizontal forgiveness, I have done all that you want me to do. But if not, right now I release the penalty of his offense to You."

But if a believer understands vertical forgiveness, and if he is obedient in releasing to God the penalties of all offenses, how could an offender possibly come to him asking for forgiveness before he has *(or should have)* released to God the penalty of the offense? The answer is simple— only if he did not know of the offense until his offender revealed it to him.

If believers use vertical forgiveness regularly and promptly, it will be a rare occasion indeed when an offender is asked to grant horizontal forgiveness before he has released to God the penalty of the offense through vertical forgiveness.

Who Needs Vertical Forgiveness?

Who needs the power of vertical forgiveness? Every believer. Being surrounded by unbelievers as well as by believers whose walk *(like yours and mine)* is not without sin, every believer needs vertical forgiveness. And every believer should avail himself of the power of vertical forgiveness every time he thinks he has been offended.

Who Needs Horizontal Forgiveness?

Who needs horizontal forgiveness? Offenders do. Lawrence needed horizontal forgiveness. He needed it to help Marvin. Under God, he was responsible to repent of his sin and to help Marvin by asking him for forgiveness.

Offenders, whether believers or unbelievers, need the power of horizontal forgiveness to help those they offend. Lawrence needed the power of horizontal forgiveness to help the one he had offended— Marvin.

Perhaps Lawrence was too proud or too stubborn to ask Marvin to forgive him. Marvin, however, should not have been dependent upon Lawrence's asking him for forgiveness. Marvin was a believer. He could have used vertical forgiveness.

Believers who understand vertical forgiveness do not need the power of horizontal forgiveness to heal wounds they receive from offenders. Instead, believers have the power of vertical forgiveness— praying and unconditionally releasing to God the penalty of each offense.

If Marvin had understood vertical forgiveness, he could have taken care of Lawrence's offense by releasing to God the penalty of the offense. Then, not needing horizontal forgiveness to obtain relief from angry or hurt feelings, he could have used horizontal forgiveness to help Lawrence— the one who offended him.

After praying and turning over to God the penalty of Lawrence's offense, he could have ministered to the one who had hurt him. Marvin could have confronted Lawrence for the purposes of restoring fellowship between them and bringing him back into fellowship with God.

When the offended person is a believer who understands vertical forgiveness, he can handle the offense by releasing to God the penalty of the offense *(vertical forgiveness)*, and then he can rebuke the offender— for the offender's good— for the purpose of bringing the offender to repentance.

But when the offended person is an unbeliever or a believer who doesn't understand vertical forgiveness, he needs horizontal forgiveness to relieve him of his angry or hurt feelings. He needs the help of another person— help that he may or may not receive. He is helpless— hoping that someday the offender may repent. Imagine. A believer who does not understand vertical forgiveness is as helpless in overcoming offenses as an unbeliever!

The offender, whether believer or unbeliever, needs horizontal forgiveness to relieve his conscience. It is the will of God that he go to the one he has offended and seek to help the one he has hurt, making restitution if such is appropriate.

If a believer has offended another believer, the offended believer *(after he has used vertical forgiveness)* should rebuke the offender with the goals of restoring fellowship between them and bringing the offending believer back into fellowship with God.

If an unbeliever has offended a believer, the offended believer *(after using vertical forgiveness)* should rebuke the offender *(if he believes that he can help the offender in doing so)* with the goal of bringing the offending unbeliever to repentance and saving faith.

Released from What?

Now for a few nuts and bolts of horizontal forgiveness. I don't know the original source of all of these principles of horizontal forgiveness, but I do appreciate the contributions of those who developed them and also those who taught them to me.[1] After teaching horizontal forgiveness to many others over the years, I am not sure which things I have added.

First of all, horizontal forgiveness is a verbal contract. The one asking for forgiveness must specify the offenses from which he wants to be released, and he must state the way he wants to be released. If someone should say, "Please forgive me for cheating," is he asking to be forgiven for the **fact** of cheating *(for the act of defrauding)*, or does he also want to be released from the responsibility of repayment *(restitution)*?

Restitution

If the offender really is repentant, and if restitution is possible, will he ask to be released from doing the godly thing? Will he ask to be relieved from repayment? John the Baptist admonished the Pharisees and Sadducees to "bring forth fruits worthy of repentance" (Matt. 3:8).

If an offender's supposed repentance seems fraudulent because of an unwillingness to make reasonable restitution, is it an act of love to grant his request for horizontal forgiveness? No. It may be an act of ignorance or cowardice. Whatever it is, it is not an act of *agape* love.

Know Before You Say "Yes"

Love does what is best for the other person. What is best for him? Is it best for him to have his conscience relieved by your granting him horizontal forgiveness when his repentance is insincere, or is it best to leave him under God's pressure?

If the offender does not make clear what he wants to be forgiven, as it comes to his mind later he will not know what has been forgiven. And if he has not made his request clear, the offended person will not know what he has released. Neither person will know what has been forgiven unless the offender states his request clearly and unless the offended person states that he is granting the entire request, a part of the request, or none of it.

This is of utmost importance: fact must take precedence over feelings. It is not a prerequisite to **either** vertical forgiveness of the penalty of an offense through prayer **or** granting horizontal forgiveness to a repentant offender to feel like forgiving. Having a "spirit of forgiveness" *(whatever that is)* is not necessary. Instead, granting horizontal forgiveness to a repentant offender is an act of the will. After horizontal forgiveness has been granted, fact again must take precedence over feeling. If you have said, "Yes, I forgive you," you **have** forgiven whether you feel like it or not.

Be Controlled by Facts

After granting horizontal forgiveness, the words that you speak must be controlled by the **fact** of forgiveness. You must refrain from saying anything vengeful to anyone about the offender. This includes gossip.

Instead of sinning with your mouth, if you feel badly toward the forgiven offender, question yourself, "Have I released to God the penalty of the offense? Or is the penalty of the offense still stuck in my heart?" Perhaps you will need to use vertical forgiveness before your heart is at peace.

Also obey God by loving the offender that you have forgiven— do good for him, say good about him, and pray for him (Luke 6:27-28). Sooner or later, God will change your feelings toward him.

When You Are the Offender

If you are the offender and need to get right with someone— and at times you will— be careful to do it correctly. Ask in a way that will help the other person the most. Ask for forgiveness in the way that will most nearly remove any stumbling block that you have placed in his path— whether this stumbling block be a hindrance to his salvation or a hindrance to his fellowship with God.

Use Wisdom and Discretion

Whether you are the offender or are confronting the offender, choose the right time, the right place, the right audience, and the right method of communication.

Letters are poor because, by either procrastination or intent, they may not be answered. Also, letters tend to prevent the give and take of dialogue that might clear up a misunderstanding. In addition, under certain circumstances, letters could fall into the wrong hands and cause trouble or embarrassment for you, for the one you have offended, or for others.

Telephone calls are better, but if overheard or recorded, could be a source of future trouble.

Personal conversations are usually best, but unless carefully planned and conducted, could damage someone's reputation, strain formerly friendly relationships, or be physically harmful.

Interruptions can prevent successfully confessing one's error and receiving forgiveness from the offended. Less-than-confidential situations can lead to damaging gossip. Whether you are the offender or the offended, be careful that you help, not harm, the other person. Keep the circle of knowledge as small as possible. Choose when, how, and where carefully.

And don't forget to consider—love and wisdom may dictate not confronting your offender at all, but instead, leaving it in the hands of the Lord.

State Your Offense Clearly

If you are the offender, be sure that you state your error clearly *(but discreetly—Eph. 4:29)*, and be sure that the one you have offended knows that you are repentant. You will be asking him to release you from your wrong action and possibly from repayment of a debt. Unless you state your offense clearly, if he says, "Yes, I forgive you," will either of you know what has been forgiven?

A Longer List Than Yours?

A word of caution: the person who offended you may have a mental list of your offenses against him. His list may include things that you don't consider offenses or things that you are confident you didn't do. If so, you may consider his accusations offensive and react in an ungodly manner. Be ready to use vertical forgiveness so that you will be prepared to answer softly if you feel he is attacking you (Prov. 15:1). Pray and release to God the penalty of the other person's offense while he is yet speaking.

Be Careful

Avoid blame-shifting or even attempting to place any blame on the person you offended. If you say, "Please forgive me for the way I reacted to you," you are blaming him, implying that if he hadn't acted in a given manner you wouldn't have responded sinfully.

Be sure to say, "Will you forgive me?" It is not enough to say that you are sorry. If you only say you are sorry, the offended person may express his regret that you offended him. Instead of expressing his regret, the offended person needs to release you. He needs to say, "Yes, I forgive you."

Don't be deceived. If he says, "It's all right," he may be attempting to avoid saying those words which would help him most. Try again. Say, "No, this is important. I have offended you. Will you forgive me?"

Do not allow the offended person to get off the hook by trying to accept part of the blame. Sometimes it is easier for him to accept a small part of the guilt than to grant forgiveness.

One Hundred Percent Guilty

But perhaps he did have some guilt in the problem between you. If so, you are one hundred percent guilty for your offense, and he is one hundred percent guilty for his offense. You should say, "No, I am entirely guilty for what I did, and I am asking you to forgive me. After granting me forgiveness, if you want to ask me for forgiveness for anything, fine, I will be willing to listen. But for now, I have acknowledged my guilt, I have expressed my repentance, and I have asked for forgiveness. Will you forgive me?"

Help Him

If you have offended a believer, ask his forgiveness. It may be that he lacks the knowledge of vertical forgiveness or the will to obey God by praying and unconditionally forgiving your offense. If so, your request for horizontal forgiveness can help him overcome the wound of your offense, and it may help him in his walk with God.

If you have offended a believer, even if he has handled it biblically between himself and God by vertical forgiveness, your attempt to "get right" with him can still help him. It can help him overcome any bad feelings he may still have against you. Your biblical example may help him to help others by asking their forgiveness, even as you have helped him.

If you have offended an unbeliever, ask his forgiveness. It may be that your offense was driving him away from God and salvation. It may be that others were driven away from God and salvation as they heard of your offense. Your godly example, in trying to help him by asking for forgiveness, may help others become Christians.

Whether you have offended a believer or an unbeliever, someone who loves him may have taken your offense as being an offense against himself. It may be that your offense is driving this loved one away from either salvation or fellowship with God. In trying to help the one you have offended, your godly action may help others that you have not even met.

If you have been offended, after you have prayed and released the penalty of his offense, if it is for his good, go and tell the offender of his offense. In doing so, you may help him by giving him a specific time and occasion to do what is right— to do what God wants him to do— to get right with God by getting right with you (Matt. 5:23-24, 18:15-16; Mark 11:25; Luke 17:3-4).

Basic Principles

The relationship between horizontal forgiveness of offenders and vertical forgiveness and their uses are governed by these principles:

- Vertical forgiveness: This kind of forgiveness is for offended believers— releasing to God the penalty of the offense brings relief to them. Believers who understand vertical forgiveness are not dependent upon repentance of their offenders *(to receive relief from angry or hurt feelings)*, but their offenders still have the obligation of asking them for forgiveness.

- Confronting and rebuking: It is the duty of offended believers to confront their offenders. If the offender is a believer, the goal of the offended believer is for the offender to: (1) repent and ask for forgiveness; (2) make restitution if appropriate; (3) be restored to fellowship with the one he has offended; and (4) be restored to fellowship with God. And if the offender is an unbeliever, the goal of the offended believer is to minister to the unbeliever with the Gospel.

- Repenting and making restitution: Repentance is a prerequisite for receiving horizontal forgiveness, and when appropriate, making restitution is also a prerequisite.

- Requesting horizontal forgiveness: It is the duty of offending believers to ask for forgiveness from those whom they offend, whether the offended person is a believer or an unbeliever. Requests for forgiveness must clearly state what is asked. Is the offender requesting to be released from the alienation that his offense caused, or is the offender also asking that he be released from paying a just debt or making restitution?

- Granting horizontal forgiveness: Responding to a request for horizontal forgiveness by granting horizontal forgiveness helps release stress from the offended person. This kind of forgiveness is helpful to all who are offended, but two groups need it most: believers who do not understand vertical forgiveness and unbelievers. When he grants horizontal forgiveness, the offended person should state clearly whether all or a part of the request is being granted.

- Withholding as an act of love: Loving an offender means withholding horizontal forgiveness when his present performance contradicts his alleged repentance. And loving an offender means withholding horizontal forgiveness when an offender should, but refuses to, make restitution.

- Granting graciously: When the offender is eligible for horizontal forgiveness *(because of repentance, with or without restitution)* horizontal forgiveness should be granted graciously.

- The principle of love: *Agape* love means doing what is best for another— this is the governing principle.

A Better Power Than "Maybe"

Horizontal forgiveness is important, and it has power to help others. But its power is limited. Since man has a sin nature, the path to success in using horizontal forgiveness is strewn with "maybe's." Maybe tomorrow he will repent. Maybe someday he will repent. Maybe.

Maybe the offender will have concern for the one he has offended, will swallow his pride, and will get right with him. Maybe, if confronted, the offender will be willing to listen and repent. Maybe the offended and offender will agree on what happened. Maybe the offender still lives in the same geographical area. Maybe he is still alive. Maybe horizontal forgiveness will work. But it is weak in sinful flesh. Too often it does not work.

As believers, we have the power of vertical forgiveness. We can find relief from the offenses of others by releasing to God promptly the penalty of each offense. And as believers, we have the God-given responsibility to use horizontal forgiveness to help others, both when we are offended and when we are the offender.

———

Summary

People are staggering and falling from the wounds of offenses they have received from others. They are failing in the Christian walk. Many of these believers are out of fellowship with God; some have left the church.

God has provided both vertical forgiveness *(unconditional release to God of the penalty of each offense)* and horizontal forgiveness *(release from estrangement between the offended and his offender)* to heal wounds resulting from offenses.

Vertical forgiveness is upward in direction— the offended person releasing to God the penalty of the offense. Horizontal forgiveness, as its name indicates, is between individuals— the offended releasing the offender from his offense.

Vertical forgiveness has the greatest power— the power of God. In contrast, the weakness of horizontal forgiveness is the sinfulness of human nature.

Horizontal forgiveness is important, too. Helping others to both walk in fellowship with God and find release from their emotional distress *(such as anger)* are the primary purposes of horizontal forgiveness.

But some people need horizontal forgiveness to receive relief from offenses against them. Three groups of people need it: (1) unbelievers; (2) believers who refuse to obey God and forgive unconditionally; and (3) believers who do not know that they can pray and unconditionally release to God the penalty of offenses against them.

Isn't it ironic? If a believer is offended by an unbeliever, and the believer is either uninformed or unwilling to use vertical forgiveness *(to release to God the penalty of the offense)*, he is at the mercy of an unbeliever.

Think of it! He— a child of God— is dependent upon an unbeliever to come to him and ask for forgiveness to help him overcome his anger or hurt feelings.

Some of the nuts and bolts of horizontal forgiveness include:

- Whether you are the offender or the offended person, choose the right time, the right place, the right audience *(between you and him alone, if it is both safe and appropriate)*, and the right kind of communication.

- If you are the offender, be sure that the offended person knows that you are repentant, how you propose to make restitution *(if appropriate)*, and exactly what you are asking the offended person to release when he grants horizontal forgiveness *(release from alienation caused by his offense, and perhaps also release from making restitution)*.

- If you are the offender, avoid blame-shifting and be sure that you actually ask for forgiveness, rather than merely expressing sorrow.

- Gently insist on a response to your request for horizontal forgiveness, and don't allow the offended person to avoid responding by trying to share the guilt with you. After granting your request for vertical forgiveness, if he is guilty of offending you, he can ask you to forgive him.

As a believer, you have the power of vertical forgiveness. You can release to God the penalty of each offense, and He will heal your wounds. Then use the power of horizontal forgiveness to help others.

Chapter Ten

Overcoming Enemy Control

Jim *(not his real name)*, a professing Christian, had tried to commit suicide. One of his high school teachers had been treating him badly. With eagerness for revenge, he told me the ways he had considered getting even.

After listening to his story I said, "If I were you, I wouldn't let him do that to me!" From then on, I had his rapt attention.

"Jim, you are letting your enemy control you. You are letting that teacher control your behavior. He is controlling your desire to make good grades *(which might affect future scholarships)*, and in the despondence precipitated by your anger at your teacher, you almost took your own life!

"In the way you reacted, you have tarnished your Christian witness. By your behavior, you have hurt your parents whom you love dearly. You have been gloomy and short-tempered with your best friends. Quite likely, because of your anger, your body is not functioning as it should. Worst of all, you are letting that teacher keep you out of fellowship with God. You are letting your teacher 'cut the telephone line' between you and God."

I explained to him that he must pray and unconditionally forgive the penalty of each offense of his teacher *(vertical forgiveness)*. If he didn't, he would be letting his "enemy" keep him out of fellowship with God (Mark 11:25 and Matt. 6:15).

"Surely, Jim, you would not want to let your enemy keep you out of fellowship with God. Surely you would not want your unforgiveness to keep God from listening to your prayers" (Ps. 66:18).

Jim was letting his teacher's offenses interfere with his relationship with God. What about you? And what about your emotional control? Is your enemy controlling your emotions? Are you behaving in an ungodly manner toward those whom you love because you are angry or bitter toward your enemy?

You may say that you don't dislike that person, or you may even say that you love him— but do you feel uncomfortable around him? Do you go out of your way to avoid meeting him face to face?

Feelings Are Not Sinful

You may not have thought of it this way, and it may surprise you, but your feelings of anger or bitterness are not necessarily sin. Paul says, "Be angry, and do not sin . . ." (Eph. 4:26). Paraphrased, this verse says, "So you have angry feelings toward someone— exert self-control and do not act sinfully. The fact that you have bad feelings toward someone is not in itself a sin."

As someone has said, "Feelings are like the indicator lights on the dashboard of your car. When one of the lights comes on, it is working exactly as it should. The solution is not to cover the indicator light so that you can't see it, nor to destroy the bulb. Instead, the solution is to look under the hood to find the problem."[1]

When you have feelings of bitterness, wrath, or anger, the problem is not your feelings. Your emotions are

working exactly as God designed them— it is His provision for making you aware of problems. Your feelings
are merely indicators showing you that a problem exists
within you.

The emotion of anger tells us to evaluate the situation
that underlies the emotion. Anger should raise the questions: What is wrong? Has someone done something
to me? Who has done it, and what has he done? What
should I do? Run? Fight? Use vertical forgiveness?

You Cannot Control Your Feelings

Feelings such as bitterness, wrath, and anger are
not volitionally controllable. It is not in your power to
change your feelings by simple acts of the will. Your
feelings merely reflect a situation, or an imaginary
situation, as you perceive it.

As you will remember, some erroneously teach that
God's command to unconditionally release to Him the
penalties of the offenses of others *(vertical forgiveness)*,
as taught in Mark 11:25, merely means believers must
have a "spirit of forgiveness" and "be willing to forgive
if ever asked."

This erroneous interpretation of our Lord's teaching
on forgiveness presents a real problem. If you are bitter
or angry, you cannot control these feelings by acts of
the will. Since your feelings are not volitional, it is impossible to force yourself to have a spirit *(feeling)* of
forgiveness.

Thus the teaching that believers cannot forgive
unless asked by the offender leaves a bitter or angry
Christian devoid of the power of forgiveness. It leaves
him without any remedy except trying in vain to per-
suade himself *(against his better knowledge)* that he is
not bitter or angry.

Obey! You Do Not Have to "Feel"

However, if we realize that God's command to pray and unconditionally forgive the penalties of offenses against us is a command to be obeyed, and not merely a suggestion that we conjure up a feeling, then we are able to use the power of vertical forgiveness (Mark 11:25). We are able to overcome "enemy control" of our emotions.

Let God Do It

This power to overcome enemy control of our emotions is taught in Ephesians 4:31-32. In verse 31 we read, "Let all bitterness and wrath and anger and clamor and slander be put away from you, along with all malice" (Eph. 4:31 NASB).

This is **not** a command **for us** to put away these things. Instead it is a command to let God do it.

At least two versions of the New Testament translate Ephesians 4:31, "Get rid of all . . . ," but most versions translate, "Let all . . . be put away from you." The Greek text will allow either translation, but when we realize that feelings are not volitional, "Get rid of all . . ." does not make good sense.[2-8]

"Get rid of" gives the erroneous implication that it is up to man to change his feelings— but it is impossible to volitionally change one's feelings. Feelings are a result of what is going on inside a person— an indicator of how he is acting and/or reacting.

Some might point to the "clamor" *("excited arguing")* and "slander" in Ephesians 4:31 and say, "Those are volitional— all you have to do to control them is to close your mouth." This is true. But if God puts away the bad heart attitude it is not necessary to clamp one's mouth shut to prevent this sinful behavior. God puts away these volitional actions by changing the heart—by taking away the pressure driving the believer toward sinful outbursts.

Ephesians 4:31 is a command to let God put away bad feelings. It is also a command to let Him put away the bad heart attitude that could cause sinful words, such as excited arguing or slander.[9-11]

What Must We Do?

But what must we do to let Him put away these things? God has provided the answer in Ephesians 4:32: "And[12-15] be kind to one another, tenderhearted, forgiving one another, even as God in Christ forgave you." The way to "let God put away" bad feelings is to obey His command to forgive. But how are we to forgive: **conditionally** *(horizontal forgiveness)* when our offender repents, or **unconditionally** releasing to God the penalty of the offense *(vertical forgiveness)*?

As God Has Forgiven Us

According to Ephesians 4:32, we are to forgive **"as"** — in the same way as— God has forgiven us. But God has forgiven us in two ways. He forgave us at the time of our justification, and this forgiveness of our sins was conditional. It was dependent upon saving faith. He also has forgiven us unconditionally, time after time, since we have been saved, as taught in 1 John 2:1. Which is meant here? If we are to take this verse seriously, we must know.

Does Ephesians 4:32 teach that we are to forgive others conditionally *(if and when our offenders repent)*, **as** God forgave us conditionally **at** the of our saving faith and justification? Or are we to forgive the penalties of the offenses of others unconditionally, **as** God has unconditionally forgiven us, time after time, **since** we were justified?

Some popular versions translate Ephesians 4:32: "as God . . . forgave you." Translated this way, this verse seems to refer to a **single event** of God's forgiveness in past time.

If verse 32 does refer to a single event of God's forgiveness of us in past time, then this verse must be referring to God's conditional forgiveness of us at the time of our saving faith and justification. Therefore, since our forgiveness of others is to be **like** *(as)* God's forgiveness of us, if this translation of verse 32 is correct, then we are to forgive others conditionally, using horizontal forgiveness, **if** and **when** those who offend us repent. We can paraphrase, "forgiving those who offend you conditionally *[when they repent]*, **even as** God's initial judicial forgiveness of your sins was dependent upon your saving faith."

In contrast, the New American Standard Bible translates Ephesians 4:32: "as God . . . has forgiven you." In like manner, the King James Version translates: "as God . . . hath *[has]* forgiven you."

While "as God forgave you" seems to limit God's forgiveness to a single event in past time, "as God has forgiven you" can be understood to include **any** number of events in past time. Thus, "as God . . . has forgiven you" can be understood to be God's **unconditional** forgiveness of us **each** and **every** time we have sinned since we were saved. If this interpretation is correct, since our forgiveness of others is to be **as** *(in the same way that)* God has forgiven us, Ephesians 4:32 teaches that our forgiveness must be **unconditional** *(vertical forgiveness)* when we are offended by others.

A paraphrase of Ephesians 4:32 that incorporates the truth of 1 John 2:1 may be helpful: ". . . unconditionally releasing to God the penalties of one another's offenses time after time *[whether or not those who offend us repent and ask to be forgiven]* **even as** God in Christ has unconditionally forgiven us time after time since the moment of our saving faith and justification *[whether or not we have been repentant, and whether or not we have confessed our sins]*."

Which Translation Is Correct?

Which translation is correct: "as God forgave you," or "as God has forgiven you"? The original language of the New Testament will allow either.[16-18] Further, we cannot determine which translation is correct from theology, because God provides two kinds of judicial forgiveness. He grants initial judicial forgiveness that is conditional *(to unbelievers at the moment of saving faith and justification), and He provides repetitive judicial forgiveness that is unconditional (to believers upon every occasion of sin).*

Let Context Decide

Is God's forgiveness in Ephesians His initial judicial forgiveness that is conditional *(dependent upon saving faith)*, or is it His repetitive judicial forgiveness that is unconditional? We must look to the context to decide.

Follow this reasoning with me:

- In Ephesians 4:31, God commands that we let **Him** put away **all** bitterness, anger, and wrath.

- We are to let Him put away **all** of these bad feelings **by** forgiving others (Eph. 4:32).

- However, **not all** offenders will repent.

- **Not all** offenders can be forgiven with horizontal forgiveness, since this kind of forgiveness is dependent upon repentance (Luke 17:3-4).

- Therefore, to be able to obey God's command to let Him put away **all** bitterness, wrath, and anger, our forgiveness of others must be vertical forgiveness, which is unconditional (Mark 11:25).

- And, since our forgiveness is to be **like** *(as)* God's forgiveness, His forgiveness in Ephesians 4:32 is unconditional *(the repetitive judicial forgiveness of 1 John 2:1)*.

It is impossible to understand "Let all bitterness, wrath, anger . . . be put away from you" to be teaching that we wait to forgive until, possibly, someday, the one who has offended us will repent (Eph. 4:31).

Therefore, as made evident by the context, for our forgiveness to be like God's forgiveness of Ephesians 4:32, our forgiveness of others must be unconditional. It must be vertical forgiveness— unconditionally releasing to God the penalty of each offense.

Look to the Context Again

But if we were to wait, how long should we wait? Again we look to context. We are to take care of our wrath "before the sun goes down" (Eph. 4:26). Follow this logic with me:

- We are to take care of our wrath **before** the sun goes down.

- Some who offend us will **never** repent and ask us to forgive them.

- An even larger percentage of offenders **will not** repent and ask us for forgiveness **before** the sun goes down (Eph. 4:26).

- **To keep** the sun from going down on our wrath, Ephesians 4:31 must be teaching vertical forgiveness— unconditional release to God of the penalty of each offense.

- Therefore, God's forgiveness in Ephesians 4:32 must be His repetitive judicial forgiveness (*the repetitive judicial forgiveness of 1 John 2:1*).

Again we see that Ephesians 4:32 teaches that our forgiveness must be vertical forgiveness— unconditional release to God of the penalty of each offense against us.

What do you think? Isn't it foolish to think that we can **always** obey the command to not let the sun go down on our wrath if we insist on waiting, perhaps in vain, for an offender to come to us and say that he repents?

It Should Be Clear

Thus we conclude that there are two arguments from context showing that Ephesians 4:32 teaches that we must unconditionally forgive the penalties of offenses against us:

- We **are** to let God put away **all** bitterness, wrath, and anger— even though **not all** offenders will repent.

- We are **not** to let the sun go down on our wrath, even though many offenders will **not** repent that soon, and others will **never** repent.

Thus, it is doubly clear by the context that "as God . . . has forgiven you" (NASB) and "as God . . . hath *[has]* forgiven you" (KJV) both allow us to correctly understand that Ephesians 4:32 refers to God's unconditional forgiveness *(repetitive judicial forgiveness)* of us and our unconditional forgiveness *(vertical forgiveness)* of the penalties of the offenses of others.[19-27]

But could it be that the Holy Spirit meant for us to understand Ephesians 4:32 to include both our horizontal forgiveness of others as well as our vertical forgiveness of the penalty of others' offenses against us? Perhaps. But letting God put away **all** bitterness, anger, wrath, clamor, and evil speaking demands that vertical forgiveness be the primary thrust of Ephesians 4:32. In addition, the admonition that we not let the sun go down on our anger also shows that vertical forgiveness is the primary teaching of Ephesians 4:32.

Logic in Colossians

In Colossians 3:13, our forgiveness is to be **as** *(like)* Christ's forgiveness of us. But which kind of God's forgiveness is meant in Colossians 3:13, His initial judicial forgiveness, which is conditional *(dependent upon saving faith)* or His repetitive judicial forgiveness *(provided by our Advocate's intercession— 1 John 2:1)*, which is unconditional?

Typically, Colossians 3:13 is translated "as Christ forgave us" or "as the Lord forgave you." The use of the English past tense "forgave" would tend to make us think that God's forgiveness in this verse is His initial judicial forgiveness— a one-time event for each believer.

But what about the context? Under what conditions are we to forgive? We are to forgive **if** "anyone has a complaint against anyone" (Col. 3:13). We are not to wait until the offender repents. The only condition is **if** we have a complaint against anyone. Our forgiveness is to be unconditional. Colossians 3:13 teaches that we are to use vertical forgiveness *(unconditionally releasing to God the penalty of the offense)* whenever we have anything against anyone.

Since, by context, our forgiveness in Colossians 3:13 must be unconditional *(vertical forgiveness)*, for our forgiveness to be the same as God's forgiveness of us, His forgiveness of us in Colossians 3:13 must be His unconditional forgiveness *(repetitive judicial forgiveness— unconditional forgiveness of our sins, time after time, day after day [1 John 2:1])*.

While it is more common to translate Colossians 3:13 "as Christ forgave you" or "as the Lord forgave you," the context teaches that this verse would be more accurately translated "as Christ has forgiven you" or "as the Lord has forgiven you."

Not only does the context demand "has forgiven," but also "has forgiven" is a valid translation of the Greek text.[28]

Versions that translate Colossians 3:13 with "as the Lord has forgiven you" or "as Christ has forgiven you" help us to understand that this verse is referring to God's repetitive judicial forgiveness. And these versions help us to see that Colossians 3:13 is referring to separate acts of God's unconditional judicial forgiveness as our Advocate intercedes for us each time we sin after we have been justified.

At least six versions translate Colossians 3:13 with "has forgiven" or "has freely forgiven." Among these is The New Translation— The Letters of the New Testament[29] which translates: "Be tolerant with each other, and if you have a complaint against anyone, freely forgive just as the Lord has freely forgiven you."

Just as Mark 11:25 teaches the necessity of vertical forgiveness *(unconditionally releasing to God the penalty of the offenses of others against us)*, both Ephesians 4:31-32 and Colossians 3:13 teach vertical forgiveness. The verses in Ephesians and Colossians give further confirmation that the erroneous "have a forgiving spirit" and "you can't forgive until asked" interpretations of Mark 11:25 should be rejected.

Don't Let Your Enemy Do It

It should be enough to know that power to overcome enemy control of your emotions is in your willingness to use vertical forgiveness, unconditionally releasing to God the penalty of each offense of others against you. However, there is even more to be gained as you obey God's command to use vertical forgiveness.

In chapter five we considered the servant who had been forgiven a debt so huge that he never could have repaid it, but who wouldn't forgive a fellow servant who owed him a pittance (Matt. 18:23-33). Continuing His illustration and making application, Jesus says, "And his master was angry, and delivered the unforgiving servant to the tormentors. The master did this to the unforgiving servant even though his fellow servant had **not** asked to be forgiven. In like manner, My heavenly Father will chastise you, if you do not use vertical forgiveness, praying and unconditionally releasing to Him the penalty of each offense against you" (Matt. 18:34-35, paraphrased).

What do you think? Is it reasonable to let your enemy set you up for chastisement from God? It is doubtful that he will know it, but your enemy will surely deliver you to God for His chastisement if you do not obey God by **unconditionally** forgiving the penalty of each of your enemy's offenses.

Again we see the importance of realizing that Mark 11:25 does not, as some erroneously teach, command a "feeling." This verse instead teaches vertical forgiveness. It teaches that we must pray and unconditionally release to God the penalty of every offense against us.

Can Others Make You Roar?

The person who cannot control his emotions is like a lion in a cage. Mischievous boys use sticks to poke the lion through the bars, just to hear it roar. A person who cannot control his emotions is like the lion— all he can do is roar, and those who want to provoke him enjoy hearing him roar. What about you— can others make you roar by poking you with verbal sticks?

Is there some enemy who is controlling you? He may be near at hand, far away, or at an unknown location. He may be dead or alive. He may be an unbeliever, a fellow Christian, a close relative, or even your mate. You may say that you love him dearly. But is your unforgiveness making him an enemy who is controlling your fellowship with God? Do you feel as if your prayers are going no higher than the ceiling? It may be that your feelings are correct.

Is there bitterness or anger in your heart? Are you treating some loved one badly because of anger toward another person?

Is it a recent problem? Does it go back many years? Are you angry with one person and behaving badly toward him, or are you treating someone badly that you dearly love because of an offense against you by another person? Are you deceiving yourself by saying that you do not have bad feelings toward him?

Be obedient to God and use vertical forgiveness— pray, and unconditionally release to Him the penalty of the offense. Your fellowship with God may depend upon it. Your Christian witness may depend upon it. Your relationships with those you love the most may depend upon it.

After you have used vertical forgiveness, apply another biblical principle to your life. It will accelerate changing your bad feelings toward your enemy to good feelings.

Love Your "Enemy"

Jesus says, "Love your enemies . . ." (Luke 6:27). Jesus is not instructing you to "feel good" toward your enemy. Instead, as acts of the will, He commands you to dedicate yourself to doing things purposefully for your enemy's good. This is *agape* love.

Luke 6:27-28 list three ways for you to love your "enemies" *(anyone toward whom you have bad feelings)* with *agape* love.

The first way to love your enemies with *agape* love is to do kind and considerate things for them. "Do good to those who hate you" (Luke 6:27). However, this is not always appropriate. If Millie were to do kind and considerate things for Burt, he might get the wrong message. In some instances it is not prudent or even safe to do kind and considerate acts for an "enemy." If in doubt, before loving an enemy by doing kind and considerate things, obtain advice from a parent or another mature Christian.

The second way to love your enemy is to bless him. "Bless those who curse you" (Luke 6:28). Search out the good qualities in your enemy's life and say those good things to him and to others. Compliment him truthfully without flattery.

The third way to love your enemy is to "pray for those who despitefully use you" (Luke 6:28). In response to your repeated actions of *agape* love, as evidenced by your prayers for your enemy, God will change your feelings toward him. Instead of being controlled by anger, you will be concerned for him and his spiritual needs.

Let me illustrate by a personal example. I read an account in the newspaper of a man who perpetrated a horrible crime. His offense was against a certain victim and against society, rather than being against me personally. And in reality his offense was against his Creator. But I felt anger toward him.

God convicted me to pray for the offender. I loved my enemy with *agape* love by acting in a direction diametrically opposite to my feelings. As I loved my enemy with *agape* love by praying for him and his salvation, God took away my anger (Luke 6:27-28).

If you have used vertical forgiveness, praying and unconditionally releasing to God the penalty of the offense, obey Jesus in His command to love your enemy. You may not feel like it, but God does not say to love your enemies only if you feel like it. If you love your Lord, obey Him (John 14:15). Obey Him and see how your obedience will hasten a change in your feelings.

Objectives and Results

Your objective should not be to feel good, but to obey your Lord. However, God has graciously provided vertical forgiveness and the principle of "loving your enemy" for your good. Obey Him and receive the joy that sooner or later follows using the principles of vertical forgiveness and loving your enemy.

Truly, the power to overcome enemy control is a God-given power— the power of vertical forgiveness— unconditionally releasing to God the penalty of our offender's offenses.

———

Summary

If you have bad feelings toward anyone, most likely you are letting that person control you as if he were an enemy, even though you may love him dearly. It is likely that your "enemy" is controlling your relationship with God, your emotions, your Christian witness, and your relationship with others.

God has provided a way to be free from enemy control by "forgiving each other, just as God in Christ also has forgiven you" (Eph. 4:32, NASB).

But God forgives us conditionally at the moment of our saving faith and justification *(initial judicial forgiveness);* and he forgives us unconditionally *(repetitive judicial forgiveness)* for sins committed after we are justified. Which kind is meant here?

Logically, if we are to let God put away **all** bitterness, wrath, and anger, then our forgiveness must be vertical forgiveness— unconditionally releasing to God the penalty of each offense against us. Otherwise, since **not all** will repent, **not all** can be granted horizontal forgiveness, and so we would **not** be able to let God put away **all** bitterness, wrath, and anger.

In addition, we are not to let the sun go down on our wrath; so we **can't** wait, hoping that our offenders will repent and ask to be forgiven (Eph. 4:26). Therefore, as God has forgiven us unconditionally *(repetitive judicial forgiveness)* as taught in Ephesians 4:32, our forgiveness must be unconditional *(vertical forgiveness).*

If we obediently use vertical forgiveness, God will put away **all** of our bitterness, wrath, and anger. We will not be dependent upon our offender's repentance. God will give us freedom from emotional turmoil in response to our use of vertical forgiveness.

In contrast, if we do not understand that God commands vertical forgiveness, or if we are unwilling to obey God and unconditionally release to Him the penalties of all offenses against us, we have lost the power to let Him put away **all** bitterness, wrath, and anger. We have lost the power of vertical forgiveness, whose power is of God, and we must depend upon horizontal forgiveness, whose weakness is of sinful man.

Further, if we are unwilling to obey God in using vertical forgiveness, we will be subject to God's chastisement as taught in Matthew 18:34-35. How foolish it would be to allow our enemies to bring God's chastisement upon us!

If we obey Him, in response to vertical forgiveness *(unconditionally releasing to God of the penalties of offenses)* God puts away the bitterness, wrath, and anger. Not only does the act of unconditionally releasing to God the penalty of each offense overcome enemy control of feelings, it also overcomes enemy control of our fellowship with God. *(If we won't forgive, God won't grant us repetitive fellowship forgiveness.)*

To change bad feelings to good feelings more rapidly, obey Jesus in another of His commands— love your enemy *(anyone whom you have bad feelings toward)* with *agape* love by doing kind and considerate things for him, saying good things about him, and praying for him (Luke 6:27-28).

Surely the desire of your heart is that **no one** control your relationship with God, that **no one** control your Christian witness, and that **no one** control your relationships with others. Power to overcome "enemy control" is a God-given power— the power of vertical forgiveness—praying and unconditionally releasing to God the penalty of each of our offender's offenses.

Chapter Eleven

Extending the Power of Forgiveness

Extending the power of forgiveness? How can anyone extend the power of forgiveness? It can't be done. However, a more complete knowledge of vertical forgiveness *(release to God, through prayer, of the penalties of offenses)* allows Christians to extend its use to situations beyond those in which the power of forgiveness is usually taught, understood, and used.

Think back with me: forgiveness is a fact— not a feeling. When you use vertical forgiveness, you are turning over to God the penalty of the offense for Him to judge. Whether or not you feel different after using vertical forgiveness, you have released the penalty of the offense to God. You have made a binding verbal contract with God— you must treat your offender with *agape* love.

Feelings Deny the Need

The power of vertical forgiveness can be extended to situations in which feelings deny the need for forgiveness.

Susie *(not her real name)* was coming in for counseling for problems that were stagnating her Christian growth, hampering her marriage, and keeping her from having a joyful life. She told me about an offense against her by an uncle many years earlier. I asked her how she felt toward her uncle.[1]

Remember, feelings are indicators of a situation or an individual's reaction to a situation. Emotions do not always reflect truth, and biblical truth must take precedence over feelings. But feelings are an essential source of information, both for individuals and their counselors.

Susie told me that she didn't have any bad feelings toward her uncle. She insisted that she liked her uncle very much. Her feelings did not reveal a problem, and I had no reason to disbelieve her.

What then about forgiveness? Should she pray and unconditionally forgive the penalty of her uncle's offense against her? Her feelings did not reveal a need for vertical forgiveness.

But consider this important fact: Jesus does not say, "Pray and forgive when you feel an offense." Instead He says, "And when ye *[you]* stand praying, forgive, if ye *[you]* have ought *[anything]* against any: that your Father also which is in heaven may forgive you your trespasses" (Mark 11:25 KJV).

If you are still hurting— or if hurt feelings or anger still come back from time to time— your feelings are revealing a problem. Perhaps you have prayed and unconditionally released to God the penalty of the offense, but the pain has not yet gone away. Or it may be that you have not used vertical forgiveness. If you have not released to God the penalty of the offense, now is the time to do it.

Susie's feelings did not reveal a problem. But Jesus does not say "Forgive when you feel an offense." Instead He says to forgive if you have anything against anyone. Susie remembered that she had something against someone— her uncle. There remained in her mind the fact of the offense, even though the feelings *(of anger or hurt)* seemed to have disappeared.

If you have something against someone, use vertical forgiveness. Let go of it— release to God the penalty of the offense. It doesn't matter whether your feelings reveal a problem. Unless you are certain that you have prayed and released the penalty of the offense, do it now.

Neither anger nor hurt feelings are a prerequisite to the need to use vertical forgiveness. Knowing, understanding, and acting on this principle extends the power of forgiveness. It extends the power of vertical forgiveness to situations where feelings are not accurate indicators of your heart condition. Extend the power of vertical forgiveness— extend it to offenses in which feelings deny the need for forgiveness.

Self-denial of Feelings

Time has a way of "scabbing over" hurts of the past— a covering develops over the top, but there may be a festering bitterness underneath. Often a counselee will say, "Of course I have forgiven him." I ask him, "How do you know? What did you do? When did you do it?"

You may be telling yourself something like this: "Christians don't have bad feelings toward others, and I am a Christian; therefore I don't have bad feelings toward the person who offended me." This is what Susie was doing. Be sure you are not deceiving yourself.

As Susie talked more about her uncle, she said, "If I had a gun I would kill him." This was the same person who a few minutes earlier said she had no bad feelings against her uncle. In fact, previously she had said that she liked him. Extend forgiveness to cover situations in which you may be denying your feelings of anger or hurt.

Be sure that you have actually forgiven the penalties of the offenses of everyone who has offended you. Don't be lulled into thinking you have forgiven just because your feelings don't indicate a problem. Pray and release the penalties of the offenses of everyone. It won't cost you anything— it won't hurt anything— and you may be surprised at how much it helps.

Acting on facts, rather than limiting the power of vertical forgiveness to feelings, extends the power of forgiveness. It extends the power of vertical forgiveness into situations where human nature, the tendency to be feeling oriented, and the tendency to deny that we have bad feelings toward others often limit the God-given power of vertical forgiveness.

Meditations Are "Corrupt"

We all need to be careful— both individuals who have problems and counselors. The Scriptures say: "Whatever things are true, whatever things are noble, whatever things are just, whatever things are pure, whatever things are lovely, whatever things are of good report, if there is any virtue and if there is anything praiseworthy— meditate on these things" (Phil. 4:8).

It is diametrically opposite to biblical truth to encourage anyone to meditate on the offenses of others against him. It is wrong, wrong, wrong. Don't do it! I repeat, don't meditate on the offenses of others against you. Instead, use vertical forgiveness— pray and unconditionally forgive the penalties of their offenses.

To help a counselee, a counselor needs to know how the counselee is hurting and how he has been hurt in the past. But the counselor must not encourage the counselee to dwell on these things. Find the problems, pray and unconditionally forgive the penalty of the offense, and go on with life. This is God's way for you to have victory over the past.

It is like cleaning out a garbage can— do it quickly. Get rid of the spoiled food. Don't stand over the garbage can to savor the rotten smell. Find the problems, release to God the penalties of the offenses, and go on with life.

If you are hurting, and someone is encouraging you to meditate on offenses against you, don't do it. Don't participate in this unbiblical practice. Your problems may already have been made worse by bad counseling. Extend the power of forgiveness— extend it to overcome "corrupt meditations."

Offenses That May Not Have Occurred

The power of vertical forgiveness can be extended into the area of the false memory syndrome— even to offenses that may not have occurred.

Let's consider anger again— the anger that comes back to a person as he "remembers" a supposed offense of his childhood. Perhaps he remembers it. It may be that someone told him about it. Perhaps it happened to someone else. There is no way to know for sure.

Some counselors believe and teach the secular error that a "child" is locked inside every adult. This "child" has been hurt by things that he can't remember. Counselors who believe this error may, by suggestion, help you "remember" things that never happened. You may become totally convinced that an innocent person has done a great injustice to you.

The Bible says, "And when you stand praying, if you have anything against anyone, pray and unconditionally forgive the penalty of the offense" (Mark 11:25, author's paraphrase). God is saying, "If you remember any offense against you, then while you are praying, pray and unconditionally release the penalty of the offense— turn it over to Me— even if the offender is unrepentant" (Mark 11:25, author's paraphrase).

Nowhere in the Scriptures does God even suggest that you are controlled by your subconscious. Never does He say, "You have 'repressed' your memory; try to remember what happened to you." Never does He say, "Have someone help you remember." Never does He say, "Your subconscious memories are harming you, find them and deal with them, or you will never have victory in your life." Never does He say, "You must deal with the 'child' who is trapped within you, or you will never be able to live a life that pleases Me."

God says instead, "If you have anything against anyone— if it comes to mind— if you remember it, forgive" (Mark 11:25, author's paraphrase).

"Remembering" supposed offenses of early childhood can be dangerous. A person who "remembers" things that never happened can be hurt or angry for many years. The supposed victim can be emotionally and spiritually defeated for many years. The supposed victim's marriage can be destroyed, the supposed offender can be slandered, families can be divided, and an innocent person can be sent to prison.

If you have been suffering emotionally because someone put an idea into your mind and you are convinced that an offense against you really occurred, use vertical forgiveness— pray and unconditionally release to God the penalty of the offense. But perhaps you are not sure. If you are almost sure that it happened, if you think that it might have happened, or if you are almost sure that it didn't happen but cannot be absolutely sure, handle it biblically. Use vertical forgiveness. Pray, telling God that you don't really know if the supposed offense against you really occurred, but that He knows, and you are turning the matter over to Him.

By acting on this principle you can extend the power of forgiveness to things that may not have happened. Even if the supposed offense has been put into your mind by the suggestions of a counselor, you can still extend the power of vertical forgiveness to the supposed offense. Pray and unconditionally release the penalty of the offense that might have occurred.

If you have been harmed by a counselor who has implanted false memories into your mind, and if you consider his counseling an offense, use vertical forgiveness. Pray and release to God the penalty of his offense. And if his poor counseling has caused trouble in the lives of those whom you love, pray and release the penalty of that offense. If in doubt, use vertical forgiveness.[2]

Repentance of Doubtful Validity

An offender comes to you saying that he repents and asks for forgiveness. Biblically it seems that you must grant him horizontal forgiveness, but you can't really bring yourself to believe that his alleged repentance is genuine.

As taught previously, horizontal forgiveness should be granted if the offender's supposed repentance is not contradicted by his present *(not past)* behavior. However, his past behavior may leave great skepticism in your mind that he is really repentant.

It is important to extend the power of vertical forgiveness to cover situations such as this— extend it to cover repentance of doubtful validity. Extend it to situations in which you grant horizontal forgiveness in response to repentance that seems to meet biblical requirements, but that does not have the "ring" of sincerity.

Excuses of Doubtful Validity

Be careful that you don't get trapped by an offender's excuses. What if his excuse doesn't hold water? Wanting to be gracious, you may accept an excuse that seems to be counterfeit. Or you may try to tell yourself that his excuse is plausible, even though you can't convince yourself that it really is genuine.

Be reasonable, of course. Accept excuses from an offender, as is appropriate for a Christian when given a reasonable explanation. But be careful. If you are not absolutely sure that he is dealing sincerely with you, you will need to pray and release to God the penalty of any deception. God knows whether or not there is an offense. You may need to use vertical forgiveness— pray and release to God the penalty of the supposed offense.

If you verbally accept his excuse, but your mind denies the validity of his statement, have you really excused him? Have you really released him? It is more likely that you are still holding it against him. When in doubt, pray and forgive the penalty of the offense. Extend the power of vertical forgiveness to cover excuses of doubtful validity.

Excuses You Make for the Offender

Extend the power of vertical forgiveness to cover excuses you try to make for the offender.

Don't try to excuse the offender on the basis of some problem he has had in the past. Don't tell yourself, "I know the way he was brought up." Don't tell yourself, "That is just the way he is." Don't try to excuse him.

It won't work. Instead, pray and release to God the penalty of his offense.

Included in the "excuses" area is the question of motives. Don't try to understand why he did it. Most likely the reason was sin. He yielded to his sin nature. God knows whether or not he is guilty, or how much he is guilty. The wise thing to do is to pray and release to God the penalty of his offense. Let God determine why he did it and what to do about it.

Unless there is some way you can help him live a life pleasing to God, you don't have to understand him. You don't have to know why he did it. Just pray and release to God the penalty of his offense.

Offenses That Cannot Be Solved by Communication

Some counselors believe that problems can reliably be solved by communication— by talking about the problems. Even though this idea is promoted by many Christians, it has a serious flaw: it is weak and prone to failure because of the sin nature (Rom. 7:18-21).

Rather than being a biblical concept, the idea of solving problems solely *(or even primarily)* by communicating stems from the fallacious idea that all goodness and knowledge resides in man. Making the erroneous assumption of the goodness of man, it follows *(erroneously)* that problems in human interpersonal relationships can be solved by talking about them.

The truth is diametrically opposite to this humanistic idea. Sin resides in all— even though believers have a new nature with the indwelling of the Holy Spirit (Rom. 7:18-21). Therefore, it is foolish to think that problems can, without fail, be solved by communication.

Even when there is reason to believe that a problem can be solved by communication, the power of vertical forgiveness should be used before communication is attempted. And then communication need be used only if it is good for the supposed offender.

Disputed Facts

Often the results of trying to solve problems by communication are like two children: "'tis"— "'taint," "'tis"— "'taint." This is not to say that communication should never be used to solve problems, but, the most effective place to start is with vertical forgiveness.

What should be done about problems of "'tis" and "'taint"? That is an easy question. If you think he offended you in words or action, but he denies it, pray and forgive the penalty of the supposed offense. Pray and release to God the penalty of each offense he denies, offenses he might deny if confronted, things that he may have done, and things he might not have done.

When you pray and unconditionally forgive, you are turning over to God the penalty of the offense for His judgment, His punishment, or whatever He determines to do about it. For the purpose of deciding whether or not to release to God *(through prayer)* the penalty of the offense, what difference does it make whether or not the supposed offender is really guilty? God knows. You don't. Just pray and turn it over to God to judge.

Extend the power of vertical forgiveness to handle offenses that are denied or that might be denied by a supposed offender if you confronted him.

Things Perceived as Offenses

Earlier I pointed out that the power of forgiveness can be extended into the area of the unknown motive, and more recently, into the area of contested facts— the "'tis" and the "'taint." But there are two other areas of the unknown into which the power of forgiveness can be extended, both of which are similar to that of contested facts.

One of these areas is perceived offenses. In a perceived offense, it seems to one person there was an offense, but the supposed offender might not see it that way. Confronting a supposed offender about a perceived offense may escalate the problem into a contested offense. Further, in confronting the supposed offender, he may feel that you have offended him.

How much better to extend the power of vertical forgiveness in this way, releasing to God the penalty of the offense, rather than confronting a person who might deny any offense, and who might consider your confrontation an offense against him.

Unless you are convinced that you need to confront the supposed offender for his good, handle the problem between yourself and God— pray and release to Him the penalty of the perceived offense.

Imagined Offenses

Some people have a problem with imagined offenses. The power of forgiveness should be extended to cover imagined offenses. Why stir up problems with accusations and denials?

Pray instead, unconditionally releasing to God the penalty of the imagined offense, and let Him relieve you of bitterness, wrath, anger, or hurt feelings. Even though you may be sure that what you imagine is true, extend the power of vertical forgiveness to cover imagined offenses— pray and release to God the penalty of that imagined offense.

If it is later confirmed that an offense actually took place, for the good of the offender and/or the safety of others, you can take any biblical action *(confronting the offender, notifying your/his local church for purposes of church discipline, or notifying civil authorities)*.

As a result you will be at peace within yourself; and you should have the satisfaction of knowing that you pleased God by taking the path of biblical obedience. You have not done anything to damage your fellowship with the imagined offender; and you have not precluded ministering to him in the future *(even if it should mean going to the offender, to the local church, or to civil authorities)*.

Instead of accusing someone who may be innocent, or possibly damaging his reputation unjustly, you have handled the supposed offense biblically as you released to God the penalty of the imagined offense.

"He Should Have—"

What about sins of omission? In the book of James we read, "To him who knows to do good and does not do it, to him it is sin" (James 4:17). The power of vertical forgiveness can be extended to things that others should have done, but failed to do, for you. Even if his sin of omission is not really a sin, the power of vertical forgiveness needs to be extended into this area.

What if you were expecting someone to do something for you or to give you something, and that person did not meet your expectations? Perhaps he had no idea that you were expecting something from him. If so, it would be impossible for him to ask you for forgiveness. Should you confront him? If you did, he might deny that it was a sin of omission, and the situation could become a "'tis" and "'taint" confrontation.

Handling sins of omission by vertical forgiveness is far superior to confronting someone who may not know that he has failed to meet your expectations, who may deny that he has sinned, and who may be offended by your accusations.

"I Expected Him To—"

Perhaps in the eyes of God the failure of another person to meet your expectations was not a sin of omission. Or perhaps it was. It doesn't matter whether or not it was a sin. Jesus says, "And when ye *[you]* stand praying, forgive, if ye *[you]* have ought against any . . ." (Mark 11:25 KJV). The power of unconditional forgiveness can be, and must be, extended to overcome unfulfilled expectations.

Extend the power of vertical forgiveness to cover unfulfilled expectations. But a word of caution: if these expectations go unfulfilled daily, the power of vertical forgiveness should be used daily.

Irritations

The power of vertical forgiveness can be extended for use with irritations caused by annoying habits of others. Unless irritations, such as another person cracking his knuckles, are handled biblically, these unresolved offenses can pile up day after day until a molehill seems like a mountain. Don't let the pressure of irritations grow. Extend the power of vertical forgiveness to cover irritations.

Offenses against Loved Ones

Consider as an example a pastor's wife or his children who are subjected to malicious gossip. If the pastor does not pray and unconditionally release to God the penalties of the offenses, will he be able to lead his flock to spiritual victory? Or will he be defeated in his own spiritual life by some of the people he is trying to lead?

Most people, and probably you, too, are especially vulnerable to offenses against loved ones. Don't stumble here. Pray and unconditionally release to God the penalties of all offenses.

What about the offenders? What should the pastor do about them? Loving them may mean confronting them. But loving God means praying and unconditionally turning the penalties of their offenses over to God (Mark 11:25 and John 14:15). The pastor may not know the identities of all the offenders. He may never know. He may never need to know. He can have victory over their offenses through vertical forgiveness.

The Unknown Offender

The power of forgiveness can be extended to the unknown offender. Under some circumstances, the power of forgiveness must be extended to problems caused by unknown offenders. Whether or not you know the identity of the offender does not matter: God knows who he is. Whether it is gossip in the church or a violent aggression against your family, God knows, and He will judge.

In this extended power of vertical forgiveness reside hope and victory. In the mistaken idea of trying to have a spirit of forgiveness and being willing to forgive if ever asked, lie bitterness, wrath, anger, and both spiritual and emotional defeat.

If you do not know the identity of someone who has offended you or someone you love dearly, your only hope— your only chance of victory— is in the extended power of forgiveness, praying and unconditionally releasing to God the penalty of the offense.

"Offenses" That Are "Sinless"

Jesus says, "And when you stand praying, forgive, if you have anything against anyone" (Mark 11:25, author's translation). This verse says nothing about sin— only that there is something that someone did, or something that he failed to do, that you considered an offense. God says, "Release it to Me. I am the Judge. Whether or not it is a sin is for Me to determine." Extend the power of vertical forgiveness to handle "offenses" that are "sinless."[3]

Anything against Anyone

Although we have discussed more than a dozen ways to extend the uses of the power of vertical forgiveness, its power has not been extended. Instead, our discussion of these categories has served only to illuminate the uses of vertical forgiveness that are inherent in the principle Jesus teaches in Mark 11:25.

Jesus says, "Forgive if you have anything against anyone." Notice how broad this is: anything against anyone. Jesus does not limit the power of vertical forgiveness to words or actions that are sinful. Instead, He Himself extends this kind of forgiveness to anything— anything we hold against another. He does not limit the power of vertical forgiveness. We shouldn't either.

There is great power in vertical forgiveness— especially when the power of forgiveness is used as it was intended to be: extended to cover anything against anyone.

Summary

Can the power of forgiveness be extended? No, but the **use** of vertical forgiveness can be extended to cover many kinds of situations— situations in which the power of forgiveness is all too often overlooked.

Jesus says, "And when you stand praying, forgive if you have anything against anyone" (Mark 11:25, author's translation). Consider how broad this is: "anything against anyone." Vertical forgiveness should be used:

- Whenever an offense is remembered

- If the offense has not been forgiven previously

- Whether or not hurt or bad feelings accompany remembering, and even if you love and/or "feel good" toward the offender

- If you are sure he really did it, think that he did it, suspect that he did it, or imagine that he did it

- If you perceive it as an offense, but the other person may not or does not so perceive it

- If he would deny or has denied doing it

- If you granted horizontal forgiveness when the validity of his repentance seemed doubtful

- If his excuse is of doubtful validity, or if you are trying to make excuses for him

- If you thought that he should have done something, or expected him to, but he didn't

- Whether the identity of the offender is known or unknown

- If the supposed offense was against you or a loved one

- If the offense was sinful, or if you are not sure it was sinful

Warning: don't meditate on offenses against you or listen to anyone who encourages you to do it. To meditate on the offenses of others is contrary to the teachings of the Bible (Phil. 4:8).

Don't become introspective: do not "go deep down inside yourself" to find truth; do not try to discover your "hidden motives"; and do not try to find the "child" that some would say is trapped within you.

Don't let others help you "remember" things from the past— someone may help you "remember" things that never happened. You are not controlled by things you cannot remember; and you are not controlled by your subconscious. Instead, handle all offenses biblically— unconditionally releasing to God the penalties of the offenses. If there are offenses you need to handle with vertical forgiveness, God will remind you in His time.

Perhaps you or someone you love has been harmed by a counselor who encouraged you or your loved one to be introspective, who persuaded you or a loved one that Christians can be controlled by repressed memories, or who helped you or a loved one "remember" things that may not have happened. If so, pray and release the penalties of the offenses of that counselor.

If in doubt whether or not to use vertical forgiveness, take the sure path— pray and release to God the penalty of the offense. Let Him determine the offender's guilt or innocence.

Avoid a "fizzle" in your life— extend the power of vertical forgiveness.

Chapter Twelve

When Forgiveness "Doesn't Work"

Have you ever forgiven, or thought that you had— and it didn't seem to work? Have you ever tried your very best to forgive, tried to convince yourself that you had forgiven, and then found that the anger or hurt feelings were almost as great as they had been before you tried to forgive?

Have you tried again? Have you tried time after time to forgive only to find that your forgiveness "didn't work?" If so, have you ever doubted your ability to forgive?

It does seem strange— after going to great lengths to solve the puzzles of forgiveness, after extolling the great power of forgiveness, and even after teaching ways to extend the power of forgiveness— to tell you that sometimes neither vertical forgiveness nor horizontal forgiveness will "work."

Sometimes forgiveness *(vertical and/or horizontal)* will work, but only partially— sometimes forgiveness will take away only a part of the bitterness, wrath, anger, or hurt feelings. At other times, almost all of the anger or hurt feelings remain. Where is the power of forgiveness in those cases? Why does the power of forgiveness sometimes fail?

An offender may repent and horizontal forgiveness be granted him, and yet almost all of the anger and hurt feelings remain so that horizontal forgiveness seems to be ineffective. Or a believer may use the power of vertical forgiveness, praying and releasing to God the penalty of an offense to God, and yet almost all of the anger and hurt feelings remain.

Sometimes neither horizontal nor vertical forgiveness seems to work. Sometimes neither kind can work.

When Forgiveness Won't Work

Brian *(not his real name)* was only fourteen, but already he was taller, heavier, and stronger than his father. In a gentle person, physical strength is no problem and can be an asset, but Brian had what some call an anger problem. He had "a short fuse." He would become violent, thrusting his fist through the interior walls of his parents' home and destroying other property as he resorted to temper tantrums. Some would say that he was "ventilating his feelings," but in reality his parents had allowed him to develop a sinful habit of losing self-control.

As too often happens with Christian children and youth, as well as with adults, Brian had never been taught to pray and unconditionally forgive the penalties of offenses. He had not been taught to release the penalties of offenses and let God put away his anger (Eph. 4:32).

However, while Brian did need to pray and release to God the penalty of each offense against himself, praying and forgiving the penalty of each offense would **not** have taken away **all** of Brian's anger. Vertical forgiveness could not have taken away **all** of his anger. Some of his anger was beyond the power of forgiveness.

There were many things from the past that still made him flush with anger every time he thought about them. One event occurred when he was a young child. It may not have actually happened, but the picture of it was vivid in his mind. Perhaps someone told him about it. Perhaps it happened to someone else, or it may have been a figment of his imagination. Or it might be that a counselor helped him "remember" an offense that never occurred.[1] However, he was fully persuaded in his mind that the supposed event was a historical fact.

As Brian remembered the event, he had been taken to the doctor. The doctor's nurse took his temperature and then placed him into the basket of the baby scales. Brian was furious. He yelled, screamed, kicked, and tried to get out of the basket.

What was the offense? Why was he so angry? Of course, no one would expect him at his age to know that God's primary principle for handling bitterness, wrath, and anger is prayer. But what if he had prayed and unconditionally forgiven the penalty of what he considered to be an offense against him? What would he have forgiven? What was the offense?

At his young age he didn't know that his weight was below the minimum that would tip the balance of the platform scales. He thought that he was big enough to stand on the "big scales." After all, what did that nurse think he was— a baby?

Brian had been furious at the time, and thinking about the event still made him angry. He was filled with the anger resulting from similar situations through the years.

Now at the age of fourteen, he had been taught to pray and unconditionally forgive the penalty of each offense against him. What if he were to release to God the penalty of the nurse's "offense" against him? What offense? There was no offense. How much relief from his anger would Brian receive from praying and releasing the penalty of that nonexistent offense?

Brian's anger was not caused by an offense. His anger came from within. It was not caused by another person. His anger was caused by his own sinful pride.

His anger was similar to that of a man who becomes angry when his wife makes helpful suggestions or comments about the way he is driving their car. Why does a man become angry when his wife offers helpful suggestions about his driving? It is pride. Just sinful pride.

Your Emotional Balloon

Let's review some facts about feelings. Earlier I mentioned that feelings are like indicator lights on the dashboard of your car. When one of those indicator lights comes on, the light is functioning exactly as it should. The problem is not the indicator light. The problem is under the hood. In like manner, God has given feelings as indicators— indicators of things that are actually problems, and indicators of things that we perceive as problems.

Let's imagine that your emotions are represented by a number of balloons, each one representing one emotion. Let's consider just two balloons, one labeled "anger" and the other labeled "hurt feelings." There is no air in either of the balloons. These two balloons indicate that you are not experiencing any problem with either hurt feelings or anger.

Then someone says something that offends you, and suddenly your "hurt feelings balloon" is half full of air. Before long, you remember that you must use vertical forgiveness whenever you are offended. So you pray and release to God the penalty of the offense.

Almost instantly there is some relief, but even though diminished in intensity, your hurt feelings refuse to diminish further. They will not go away. Day after day, week after week, and perhaps year after year, you can push these hurt feelings down. But they remain under the surface, periodically and painfully surfacing again and again.

You try to convince yourself that you have forgiven *(released to God the penalty of the offense)*, but you are uncomfortable around the offender. You know that something is wrong. You wonder **if** you have forgiven, or if you **can** forgive.

Or perhaps it was your "anger balloon" that suddenly became engorged with air. You feel guilty because of your anger. Should you confess your anger to God as a sin? No. Your feelings of anger are not sin (Eph. 4:26). They are merely indicators of the problem. The feelings are to alert you to take appropriate action.

Wise and Foolish Actions

Should you go to the supposed offender and tell him about your feelings? Not necessarily. What would it accomplish? He may never need to know that you have been angry with him. It is **not** a sin to feel bad toward him— but it **is** a sin to treat him badly. Just be sure that you do not sin. Exert self-control (Eph. 4:26).

If you go to him prematurely— while air is still in your emotional balloon— you may cause more problems than you solve. You may not edify the other person, and you may not glorify God in your communication. Instead of saying things that will be of help to the other

person, corrupt words may come out of your mouth
(1 Cor. 10:31; Eph. 4:29).

Furthermore, it is quite likely that you will find that
you do not need to tell the other person about your anger.
You may never need to tell him. You don't have to tell
him to get relief from your anger.

Identify the Problem

Ask yourself, "Why am I angry?" Or if you have
already prayed and unconditionally released the penalty
of the offense, ask yourself, "Why has releasing the
penalty of the offense failed to take away my anger?"
It should not take too much thought for you to realize
what sin problem is causing your emotional distress.

Is it pride, selfishness, envy, jealousy, or some other
personal sin that is causing the air to remain in your
emotional balloon? With Brian, his anger was entirely
the result of his sinful pride. The nurse had done nothing
wrong. There was no offense. Neither vertical forgiveness nor horizontal forgiveness would have worked.
Neither could have worked.

Be Careful

Don't become introspective. Introspection is a waste
of time. It is unnecessary, and it can be dangerous. Take
care of things that God reveals to you through your hurt
feelings or anger. Take care of them biblically and go on
with life.

Don't try to look deep inside yourself. Only a few
moments of reflection will most likely reveal to you
whether or not some sin of yours caused a significant
part of your emotional distress. It may take a little longer
for you to identify your sin.

But don't be too concerned if you have a problem determining whether or not a personal sin is causing your emotional distress. And don't be too concerned if you cannot identify your personal sin right away. If a sin problem is standing in the way of your progressive sanctification *(growth toward godliness in your Christian walk)*, God will reveal it to you.

Powerless Power

The power of vertical forgiveness *(being able to pray and unconditionally release to God the penalty of each offense)* is a good and powerful gift of God. Vertical forgiveness is one of God's provisions for relieving problems with feelings. As a believer you have this power available for use in an instant.

You also have the power of horizontal forgiveness, although horizontal forgiveness won't work unless the other person *(the one who should repent or the one who should grant horizontal forgiveness)* is willing to make it work.

However, neither horizontal forgiveness nor vertical forgiveness *(nor both used together)* will work when the emotional distress is largely or totally caused by sin in the one who is offended.

Since forgiveness is powerless to take away hurt feelings or anger when these feelings are caused by a personal sin *(such as pride or selfishness)*, what will take away these feelings? What power has God provided to take away these angry and hurt feelings when forgiveness *(vertical and/or horizontal)* is relatively powerless?

Cleansing the Walk

In an earlier chapter we considered the teachings of 1 John 1:9. We need to study 1 John 1:9 in more detail.

"If we confess our sins, He is faithful and just to forgive us our sins and to cleanse us from all unrighteousness" (1 John 1:9).

Some Bible students have supposed that 1 John 1:9 is a salvation verse. However, since John is addressing believers, this verse cannot be a salvation verse. Bible students who have come to their erroneous conclusion apparently have not understood the relationship between 1 John 1:9 and 1 John 2:1.

As we considered 1 John 1:9 earlier, we saw that the forgiveness that God grants in response to confession of sins is His repetitive fellowship forgiveness. The forgiveness in 1 John 1:9 cannot be judicial forgiveness. God's repetitive judicial forgiveness is unconditional (1 John 2:1), whereas the forgiveness in 1 John 1:9 is dependent upon confession. This interpretation agrees with the context of 1 John 1:9. Notice the discussion of "fellowship" in 1 John 1:6-7.

In like manner, the "cleansing" of 1 John 1:9 cannot be judicial cleansing, because judicial cleansing is a priestly ministry of Jesus in which He, as our High Priest or Advocate, intercedes for us unconditionally upon the occasion of sin (Heb. 7:24-25; 1 John 2:1). Instead, the "cleansing" of 1 John 1:9 is cleansing of the Christian walk (1 John 1:6-7). This interpretation agrees with the context of 1 John 1:9. Notice "walk" in 1 John 1:6-7.

Confession and Cleansing

And what does "confess" mean? God always tells the truth, and He expects us to tell the truth. Obviously, confessing our sins cannot include calling them anything that minimizes their sinfulness. God does not accept plea bargaining.

When we tell God the truth about our sins, we are saying the same thing about them that He does. This is what confess means— to say the same thing about our sins that God does.

So "confess" in 1 John 1:9 means to say the same thing *(in the heart if not in words)* about our sins that God says. If your sin is pride, tell God that it is pride. If it is selfishness, envy, lust, or jealousy, identify it and call it by name.

Paraphrasing, 1 John 1:9 teaches: "If we confess our sins by saying the same about our sins that God does, He is faithful and just to restore our fellowship with Himself and to cleanse our walk from every kind of unrighteousness, including sins, such as pride and selfishness, that often cause hurt feelings and anger."

When your emotional discomfort is caused by a personal sin, and forgiveness *(vertical, horizontal, or both)* will not work, you can receive cleansing of your hurt or angry feelings in response to confession of sins. Included in confession of sins is God's provision to take the air out of your emotional balloon. If we confess our sins, He will cleanse our walk— including feelings such as hurt and anger.

Using the Balloon

Now back to the balloon. Let's imagine that someone, perhaps one of your parents, said something that really hurt you many years ago. As you recall that event, even after all of these years, tears still come.

Stand back and take a look. Could any of your hurt feelings have been caused by pride? Or if that offense so many years ago caused anger, was the anger caused, at least in part, by your pride? Brian's was.

You may decide that only part of your emotional distress was caused by your sins *(such as pride and/or selfishness)*. Perhaps a part of your emotional distress was caused by a real offense against you. It could be that ninety percent was caused by the offense, and only ten percent was caused by pride. Or it might have been ten percent offense and ninety percent pride. The ratios do not matter.

Remember the balloon— the balloon of your emotional distress. First pray and confess any sin of yours that may have made your feelings greater than they should have been.

Pray something like this: "Lord, You know that my feelings have been hurt deeply. I know that my hurt feelings are much bigger than the offense. What Bob said to me would not cause so much pain if it were not for my sinful pride. Lord, forgive me for my sinful pride, and cleanse me from being a proud person."

The result of your confession of sin should be an almost immediate relief of your hurt feelings.

Then, having taken care of your sin of pride affecting this part of your emotional balloon, you are now ready to use vertical forgiveness.

Pray something like this: "Lord, for what Bob did to me, I am turning the penalty of his offense over to you— I am releasing it to you. You have promised to judge and to punish offenders, and I know that you will do what is best (Rom. 12:19). Because I am releasing to You the penalty of Bob's offense, I have no right to hold his offense against him or to treat him badly. Instead, I promise to treat him with *agape* love" (Luke 6:27-28).

By now most of the air should be out of your hurt feelings balloon. But if not, pray for the other person daily until your hurt feelings are gone.

Confirm Forgiveness, Confess Each Time

Do not pray and forgive the penalty of the same offense twice. Pray instead to confirm the fact that you have already released to God the penalty of the offense. Remember, forgiveness is a fact, not a feeling. If you have prayed and forgiven the penalty of the offense, you have made a verbal contract with God.

If anger or hurt feelings return, it will be helpful to pray and tell God again that you realize that much of your problem of hurt feelings or anger was the result of your sinful pride, selfishness, envy, jealousy, or some other personal sin. Each time anger or hurt feelings return, the cause is another occurrence of that same personal sin— a sin that needs to be confessed.

Remember the example of your emotional balloons: to obtain relief from hurt feelings, bitterness, wrath, or anger, **first** pray and confess your sin— whatever makes your bad feelings larger than the offense. **Then** pray and unconditionally release to God the penalty of the offense.

When forgiveness doesn't work, remember your emotional balloons. It may be that at least part of the remaining anger or hurt feelings is caused by a personal sin. If that is the case, the path to freedom from anger or hurt feelings resides not only in the power of forgiveness but also in the cleansing power that comes from confession of sin.

Combined and Extended Power

The combined power of confession of personal sin *(such as pride or selfishness)* and vertical forgiveness *(of the penalties of offenses)* is great. The need to use these two principles together should be considered whenever there is a problem of anger or hurt feelings.

Remember the many ways that the power of forgiveness can be extended? These two biblical principles *(confession of sin and vertical forgiveness)* can be used together in any of these areas. But let's consider only one.

Whether an offense that someone has helped you "remember" really happened has no effect on the God-given power of vertical forgiveness. The power of vertical forgiveness is not dependent upon your ability to verify a supposed offense against you.

And what if the "remembered" offense against you never happened?[2] Does that affect whether or not your feelings of anger or hurt can be partially the result of a personal sin? No. If your feelings are larger than the "remembered" offense *(indicating that part of your pain is due to a personal sin of yours)*, whether or not the offense really occurred has nothing to do with your sin. If you are reacting to a supposed offense sinfully, what does it matter whether or not the supposed offense against you really happened? It doesn't change the fact of your sin.

Therefore, if someone has helped you "remember" a supposed offense, use the principles of the balloon. First, pray and confess your pride, selfishness, or whatever sin of yours is causing a part of your pain as you "remember" the supposed offense. God will cleanse you of your emotional distress when you confess your sins, whether or not the offense actually occurred.

Perhaps a simple illustration will be helpful. What if you "remembered" being ridiculed by your kindergarten teacher in front of the entire class? Would it be beyond reason to think that as much of your pain resulted from your pride as from the words your teacher spoke? "She said that to **me**. She said it in front of the entire class. I was so humiliated." Pride is causing part of the pain.

After confessing any sinful pride *(or other personal sin)* that you think could be causing some of your emotional distress, use vertical forgiveness— pray and release to God the penalty of the supposed offense. He knows whether or not it really happened— you do not need to know. The power of these two biblical principles *(confession of a personal sin and vertical forgiveness)* is effective whether or not the supposed offense really occurred.

Confronting the Innocent

If it were not for the power of vertical forgiveness, relief would be limited to confrontation of the offender and his repentance. And what if you had been helped to "remember" an offense that had not occurred? The supposed offender would not repent of an offense that never occurred, and you would be helpless.

However, with the power of vertical forgiveness, you are not dependent upon repentance of a supposed offender who may or may not be guilty.

Having the power of vertical forgiveness, and the power of confession of personal sin to handle your emotional distress, you can ask yourself, "What is good for the supposed offender?" Unless you are absolutely sure that the supposed offense really happened, how could accusing the supposed offender be considered an act of *agape* love?

Use Anytime or Every Time

When vertical forgiveness "doesn't work," look inside. The problem may be a personal sin of yours, such as pride or selfishness. If this is the case, use the power of confession of sin. Remember the balloon: to relieve emotional distress, whether real or imagined, pray and confess your personal sin and then use vertical forgiveness.

When should you consider using the combined power of confession of sin and vertical forgiveness? Consider using these two biblical principles to relieve emotional distress that results from any kind of offense, including all of the kinds of offenses that we considered in the chapter "Extending the Power of Forgiveness."

Don't overlook using these two principles to overcome the effects of the "memory" of an offense that you had *(supposedly)* repressed until someone helped you "remember." Whether or not the supposed offense really happened, the combined power of these two biblical principles will bring relief.

It is contrary to the will of God that offenses, even "memories" of offenses that may not have happened, stifle your Christian growth.

———

Summary

Emotions such as hurt feelings, anger, bitterness, and wrath are indicators, similar to the dash lights on your car. When an indicator light in your car comes on, the problem is not the light. The problem is under the hood. In like manner, hurt feelings, anger, bitterness, and wrath are God-given indicators. The feelings are not sinful; they merely indicate that a problem exists.

Anger and hurt feelings can be represented by balloons, one each for anger and hurt feelings. A part, or all, of the air in one of your emotional balloons may be due to an offense. If so, that portion of the air in your emotional balloon can be relieved by the power of vertical forgiveness— unconditionally forgiving the offense through prayer. This is one of God's gifts for handling problems of anger and hurt feelings.

However, a part or even all of the air in a person's emotional balloon may be due to a personal sin such as pride, selfishness, envy, or jealousy. Neither horizontal forgiveness, nor vertical forgiveness, nor both have the power to take away anger or hurt feelings that are caused by personal sin. Therefore, to the extent that anger or hurt feelings are caused by personal sin, forgiveness will not work.

In addition to the power of forgiveness, confession of sins is another gift of God for handling anger and hurt feelings. "If we confess our sins, He is faithful and just to forgive us our sins *(restore us to fellowship with Himself)* and to cleanse our walk *(manner of life)* from every kind of unrighteousness— including sins that often cause hurt feelings and anger, such as pride and selfishness" (1 John 1:9, paraphrased).

Therefore God's provisions for handling hurt feelings, wrath, bitterness, and anger include:

- Praying, confessing the personal sin that makes the feelings larger than the offense

- Praying, unconditionally releasing to God the penalty of the offense *(vertical forgiveness)*

When forgiveness doesn't work— perhaps along with the need to pray and unconditionally forgive the penalty of the offense, your emotional balloon indicates a personal sin to identify and confess. Ask yourself, "Is my pride, selfishness, or jealousy causing at least a part of my problem?"

Don't become introspective and try to go deep within yourself— that is unnecessary, and it can be dangerous. Within a few seconds you will most likely be able to ascertain whether a personal sin caused a substantial part of your emotional distress and to identify your sin.

This chapter teaches God-given principles for letting the air out of your emotional balloons. These principles provide power for overcoming anger or hurt feelings when forgiveness doesn't work.

Use the combined power of these two biblical principles *(confession of personal sin and vertical forgiveness)* to deflate your emotional balloons. Use these two biblical principles for any kind of offense, including "repressed memories"— memories of offenses that may or may not have happened. Whether an offense that you have been helped to "remember" really happened or not, the combined power of these two biblical principles will bring relief.

Using the God-given principles taught in this chapter, you can overcome the effect of offenses, whether real or only "memories" of things that might have happened.

Chapter Thirteen

Forgive Yourself?

She was tall, slender, and gracious. Her black hair, devoid of any gray, belied the fact that she was approaching retirement. Joan *(not her real name)* was a picture of serenity as she sat across the desk from me, but I soon discovered that in her spirit she was burdened, almost tortured, by a deep sense of guilt.

During our first counseling session she revealed a secret— a sin of her early childhood that she had hidden from everyone— a sin that had left her with a deep feeling of guilt. She described it as a knife piercing her soul.

Joan knew that Jesus had interceded for every one of her sins unconditionally, and because He had interceded for every one of her sins, He had kept her positionally righteous *(all sins paid in full)* since the moment of her saving faith and justification. That is, she had received God's repetitive judicial forgiveness as Jesus interceded for her unconditionally (1 John 2:1).

She was confident that she had confessed this sin of her childhood, and she believed that, in response to her confession, God had granted her His repetitive fellowship forgiveness (1 John 1:9).

But guilt feelings continued to torture her. What was wrong? What was missing? Could it be that she needed to forgive herself? Some would think so.

But there is a problem with the theory of forgiving oneself. Even though the Bible teaches much about forgiveness, the idea of forgiving oneself is never mentioned. The Scriptures teach instead that all sin is against the Creator, not against oneself. King David expressed this truth when he prayed, "Against You, You only, have I sinned, and done this evil in Your sight . . ." (Ps. 51:4).

Joan's need was not to forgive herself. But what could she do to find relief from her oppressive feeling of guilt?

Confession of Sins

Could it be that she had not really confessed her sin to God? Or could it be that, somehow, she failed to confess it correctly? If so, could it be that God had not granted her repetitive fellowship forgiveness? If her feelings accurately reflected truth, then He had not forgiven her. But had He?

By the way it is constructed, the Greek word that is translated "confess" in 1 John 1:9 might mean "to say the same."[1] But is this what "confess" really means?

Ordinarily, word meaning is determined by word usage. But in this instance word meaning is determined by theology. Simple logic confirms that theology does indeed teach that the Greek word translated "confess" in 1 John 1:9 means "to say the same" as God says about our sins.

The logic of understanding the meaning of "confess" in 1 John 1:9 is:

- God always tells the truth.

- He hates lies.

- When He says "confess," He means "tell the truth."

- Therefore, since God always tells the truth and He expects us to tell the truth, "confess" means "to say the same" about our sins that God says.

- That is, to "confess" a sin to God means agreeing with God about how serious the sin is, rather than trying to minimize or excuse it.

A man-in-the-street definition of "confess" might be similar to plea bargaining in civil law—a term used in pretrial negotiations in which the defendant agrees to plead guilty to a lesser charge in exchange for having more serious charges dropped. But theology tells us that we can "confess" a sin to God only by saying the same thing about it that He does.

As we discussed the problem of her guilt feelings, I came to the conclusion that Joan had really confessed her sin, and that God had granted repetitive fellowship forgiveness to her many years earlier.

Feelings or Facts

However, it bothered me that for so many years her feelings had appeared to contradict the fact of His repetitive fellowship forgiveness.

In living the Christian life, it is necessary to trust what God says, whether or not one's feelings agree with God's truth. I could have told her that sometimes feelings do not reflect truth, and sometimes even contradict it. Or I could have told her that it sometimes takes a while before feelings catch up with truth. But she would have been justified in questioning, "But so many years?"

Unless all other possible problem areas have been investigated, it can be a mistake to tell believers that their feelings have not caught up with the fact of God's forgiveness. So we kept looking for the cause of Joan's distress.

Reflected Guilt Feelings

Could it be that her godly appearance belied her behavior? Could it be that her behavior had not changed? Could it be that she was still the same sinner that she had been many years earlier?

That was a logical area to investigate. Not making biblical changes from a life of sin sometimes causes guilt feelings that focus on a past sin. The sinning Christian really believes that he is suffering from guilt of previous sins, whereas in reality a pattern of present sins is causing his guilt feelings. Then with a little erroneous teaching, it is easy for him to fall into the error of thinking that the path to relief from his guilt feelings is to forgive himself.

But investigation revealed that this was not Joan's problem. Instead, God had been working in her life to progressively sanctify her.

We investigated further. It was evident that God had made her a lovely Christian woman. With a walk that was close to her Lord, and a tender conscience, could it be some current sin causing her guilt feelings? Could it be that her guilt feeling was wrongly directed to the past?

Or could the problem be sins committed between that one childhood sin and the present? Could a sin that she committed in the intervening years be causing her emotional distress?

The Christian life is to be lived in accordance with biblical truth, rather than being guided by our senses (2 Cor. 5:7). God's Word is a compass that never errs, but our feelings may trick us. Our feelings can misguide us, even as the conscience can be wrongly conditioned (1 Cor. 8). The Scriptures teach that we should be fully persuaded *(as to right and wrong)* by our intellects *(in our minds)*, not by our feelings (Rom. 14:5b).

Sometimes a guilty conscience results from doing things that are not, in themselves, wrong. The Apostle Paul covers this problem in several passages (Rom. 14; 1 Cor. 8, 1 Cor. 10:25-29). Until fully persuaded in his own mind that a particular thing is not sinful, the believer sins and his conscience hurts *(or should hurt)* each time he fails to be faithful to his conscience (Rom. 14:5b, 22b, 23).

Obviously, a guilty conscience is likely to remain after confessing one sin, if, in fact, the guilt feeling is the result of a different sin that has not been confessed, the present practice of a sin, or of not being fully persuaded *(in one's intellect)* that a certain practice is sinless.

Again it is easy to see that forgiving self can appear to be a reasonable solution to those who are feeling the pain of a hurting conscience—especially when the emotional distress has not been relieved by confessing the sin that seemed to be causing the problem.

I became convinced that a present sin was not Joan's problem. As far as I could ascertain, while no believer lives a perfect life, she was living a life that was pleasing to her Savior. And I was almost sure that her guilt feelings did not stem from sins, or even doubtful practices, between her childhood and the present.

How Could I?

Focusing on the sin of her childhood, she was still asking herself, "Why did I do it?"

Some Christians believe that, having received a new nature, their old nature has been destroyed. Some will tell you that they never sin. But the Apostle Paul reveals that his old nature was fully active.

Paul says, "For I know that in me *[that is, in my flesh]* nothing good dwells; for to will is present with me, but how to perform what is good I do not find. For the good that I will to do, I do not do; but the evil I will not to do, that I practice" (Rom. 7:18-19).

Why had she sinned? The answer is obvious— although she was saved and God had made her a beautiful Christian— she had a depraved nature. And she had that same depraved nature when she was a child.

Not considering her depraved nature, she kept asking herself, "How could I have done such a terrible thing?" She was actually asking herself, "How could such a nice person as I am have done such a thing?" There was an element of pride in her question— and we all have an abundance of pride. There was sinful pride to confess.

She shouldn't have asked herself, "How could I have committed that sin?" Instead she should have been thanking and praising God that He, in His marvelous grace, had kept her from far worse sins.

Confession and Thanksgiving

She needed to confess her pride and thank God for saving her. She needed to praise and thank Him for causing her— a depraved individual— to will and to do His good pleasure (Phil. 2:13). She needed to transform each occasion of painful remembrance into a time of blessing by making it a time of praise and joy in the Lord.

As she confessed her sin of pride, and as she praised and thanked God, there was some relief. But much of the pain remained. Why? Why did she still have an over-whelming feeling of guilt? Were there any clues?

Delayed Guilt Feelings

She had committed this sin as a young girl, and yet the sin of her childhood did not start bothering her until she had been married for quite some time— years after the moment of her saving faith and justification, and years after she had committed that sin. After that, it was like a "knife piercing her soul" for many years.

Why had the emotional pain started so many years after the sin? For a time I was baffled about this.

Unfulfilled Expectations

She always spoke in glowing terms about her husband. Although he had not come in for counseling with her, it was abundantly clear that she had a deep love for him. The problem did not seem to be related to their marriage.

Further, in earlier counseling sessions we had talked about forgiveness. As far as I could ascertain, there were no resentments in her life against her husband or against others. I dismissed the idea that there might have been unforgiveness in her life.

But as counseling progressed, I discovered that her husband had not fulfilled all of her expectations. Perhaps it is too strong to say that she was bitter toward her be-loved husband, but there was disappointment. And yet I didn't discern any bad feelings toward him. Her gracious demeanor covered any outward manifestation of inner bitterness. She loved him dearly, she appreciated both his kindness and generosity, and she admired him— but he hadn't fulfilled all of her expectations.

It wasn't a matter of her husband's sinning. It was not as if he had done things we would ordinarily think required her forgiveness. He merely failed to fulfill all of her expectations.

Don't Excuse! Extend the Power!

So what was solution to her problem?

The answer is in extending the power of forgiveness *(see chapter eleven)*. Jesus does not say, "Forgive if you feel bitterness." And He does not say, "Forgive if it is really sinful." Of course these are included, but Jesus made it much more inclusive. He says, "Forgive if you have **anything** against **anyone**."

Joan's husband had not necessarily sinned in not meeting her expectations, and she did not have bad feelings toward him. But, for many years, she had held it against him for not meeting her expectations.

Rather than forgiving, she had been trying to excuse him by understanding him. She was telling herself, "He's a wonderful husband and I love him very much. It's not his fault that he is not meeting my expectations. That is just the way he is."

Jesus does not say, "Make excuses for those who have not met your expectations— who have failed to do something that would please you." Instead, He says, "Forgive, if ye *[you]* have ought *[anything]* against any" (Mark 11:25 KJV).

Joan had something against someone: her husband had failed to meet her expectations. Whether his failure to meet her expectations was a sin did not matter. She was holding it against him. Joan needed to forgive the

penalty of each of his offenses, not make excuses for
him.

The Problem Solved

Because she had not used vertical forgiveness—
praying and unconditionally releasing to God the
penalties of her husband's offenses *(not fulfilling
her expectations)*— she had not received God's
repetitive fellowship forgiveness.

Beware! Many Christians ensnare them themselves
in the unbiblical idea of trying to excuse others, rather
than obediently praying and releasing the penalty of the
(real, supposed, or imagined) offense.

God's fellowship forgiveness— both His initial fellowship forgiveness *(granted at the moment of saving
faith)* and His repetitive fellowship forgiveness *(granted
to believers when sins are confessed)*— could be called
"feel-like-it forgiveness." Because Joan had not prayed
and unconditionally forgiven the penalty of each *(real,
supposed, or imagined)* offense of her husband, she had
not felt God's forgiveness of her childhood sin— even
though she had confessed it many years before.

Joan did not need to forgive herself. Her childhood
sin was against God, not herself. The problem was that
she had not unconditionally released to God the penalties
of the *(supposed)* offenses of her husband. As a result,
she did not have the subjective assurance of feeling that
God had forgiven her— the gift of God for those who
will obey Him by using vertical forgiveness *(unconditionally releasing to God the penalty of each offense)*.

The Torment of Her Guilt

In the illustration that Jesus gives in Matthew 18, a
servant owed a debt so large he never could have repaid

it. Even so, he asked for more time to repay. Instead of granting more time, his master forgave him (Matt. 18:23-27). Somewhat later, a fellow servant, who owed the forgiven servant a small debt, asked for more time to repay. But the forgiven servant had his fellow servant thrown into prison (Matt. 18:23-30).

"Then his master, after he had called him, said to him, 'You wicked servant! I forgave you all that debt because you begged me *[for more time to repay, not for forgiveness]*. Should you not also have had compassion on your fellow servant *[releasing him unconditionally²]* just as I had pity on you *[just as I forgave you unconditionally]*?'" (Matt. 18:32-33)

"And his master was angry, and delivered him to the torturers until he should pay all that was due to him" (Matt. 18:34). Jesus continues by applying His illustration to those who refuse to forgive unconditionally:³ "So My heavenly Father also will do to you if each of you, from his heart, does not *[unconditionally]* forgive his brother his trespasses" (Matt. 18:35).

When Joan's husband didn't meet her expectations, she considered it a trespass against her by her husband. Whether or not it was a trespass, Mark 11:25 teaches that she should have prayed and unconditionally released to God the penalty of each *(supposed)* offense.

Her husband had not asked to be forgiven. Most likely, he didn't think he had done anything that required forgiveness. No matter. She should have prayed and unconditionally forgiven the penalty of each supposed offense.

But she did not forgive. As a result, her "torment"⁴ was a heavy feeling of guilt for a sin that she had confessed many years before. Combining the truths of Matthew 18:34-35, Jesus says, "As the master in My

illustration delivered the unforgiving servant to the torturers, in like manner, My heavenly Father will bring
distress *[chastisement]* into your life if you do not unconditionally release to Him the penalties of all offenses
against you" (paraphrased).

She hadn't forgiven. Because of this, she hadn't
received the feeling of God's forgiveness. Instead, her
guilt feelings tormented her. Because of her failure to
forgive her husband, the sin of her childhood had for
many years "pierced her like a knife in her soul."

Another Torment?

It may be that she had suffered another "torment."
She said that she didn't resent him, but I suspect that
she did at times. Most likely she masked her resentment
much of the time with good feelings toward him.

She had experienced various physical problems
through the years. Perhaps her "torment" included
psychosomatic illness— illness that starts in the mind
and results in emotions that cause real physical illness.

If some of her illnesses were psychosomatic, they
may have been God's chastisement— chastisement for
her good— to bring her to the place where she would
obediently pray and unconditionally release to God the
penalties of her husband's offenses against her (Mark
11:25; Heb. 12:6).

A Stranger to Biblical Truth

Forgive yourself? No. This idea is a stranger to biblical truth. Instead, confess your own sins, make biblical
changes in your life, and unconditionally forgive the penalties of everyone's offenses against you.

Forgiving oneself is an unbiblical exercise in futility. Instead, vertical forgiveness *(praying and unconditionally forgiving the penalty of each offense of others)* is God's will for all believers. Vertical forgiveness is God-given power that relieves the offended believer from "enemy control."

And vertical forgiveness is the biblical path for relief from guilt feelings— relief from the "torment" that is taught in Matthew 18:34-35—relief from feelings of guilt for sins that have been confessed.

Whatever you do, don't replace the power of vertical forgiveness with the fizzle of forgiving yourself. Don't do it!

———

Summary

There is one problem with the idea of forgiving yourself— it is not biblical. Sins are against God, not yourself. There is another problem with it— it won't work. It won't relieve the feelings of guilt.

Sometimes continued feelings of guilt reflect a life that has not changed. In other instances, feelings of guilt reflect a current sin, or a sin committed between that past sin and the present time, but the guilt feelings are focused on the sin of the past.

Then there is the problem of pride. There can be a deep feeling of remorse, but when a believer asks himself, "Why did I do it?" he may be asking himself, "How could such a nice person as I am have done such a terrible thing?" In cases like this, at least some of the pain stems from pride, and pride should be confessed.

At times, confession of sin does not "work"— that is, feelings of guilt continue because the believer tries to minimize or excuse his sin instead of confessing it. At times the confession is sincere, but the feeling of God's fellowship forgiveness does not immediately follow the fact of confession and God's fellowship forgiveness.

In some instances— perhaps many, many more instances than we realize, believers do **not** feel forgiven because they have **not** obeyed God and His command to use vertical forgiveness *(to pray and unconditionally release to God the penalties of everyone's offenses).*

They haven't obeyed God in using vertical forgiveness, and, because of their disobedience, God has not given them His repetitive fellowship forgiveness. As a result, they feel guilty— they have not received God's "feel-like-it forgiveness." They feel "torment," as taught in the last verse of Matthew 18— torment that comes from refusal to use vertical forgiveness.

Finally, refusal to pray and unconditionally release to God the penalties of offenses may result in psycho-somatic illness— real physical illness that stems from emotions such as resentment. This too may be a part of the torment of Matthew 18— torment that God sends to those who do not use vertical forgiveness, unconditionally releasing to Him the penalties of offenses.

Forgive yourself? No, your sins are against God. Confess them to Him. Are you holding things against others? Obediently pray and unconditionally release to God the penalties of your offender's offenses. Use the power of vertical forgiveness.

Epilogue

Power or puzzles? For those who have solved the puzzles, there is power in forgiveness—power that flows from the living God.

In solving the puzzles, we discovered that God grants four kinds of forgiveness and two other kinds are for our use—vertical forgiveness and horizontal forgiveness.

Now let's take a panoramic view of how vertical and horizontal forgiveness relate to God's prerogatives *(e.g., to reward good works and to judge sin)* and man's God-ordained responsibilities *(e.g., to maintain an orderly society)*.

God has the right to punish unbelievers for their sins, to provide both initial judicial forgiveness and repetitive judicial forgiveness, and to both bestow rewards on believers at the judgment seat of Christ and withhold them (Rom. 12:19; 1 Cor. 3:11-15; Rev. 20:11-15).

God has delegated authority to the local church to judge and to discipline those in the congregation whose behavior is contrary to biblical morality, who teach heresy, who offend others, or who otherwise bring disrepute on the name of the Lord (Matthew 18:15-17; 1 Cor. 6:1).

And God also has ordained that civil government maintain order in society by enacting laws, judging lawbreakers, and punishing them (Rom. 13:1-2).

In vertical forgiveness, the offended believer unconditionally *(without the necessity of the offender's repentance)* prays and releases to God the penalty of the offense. This volitional act of an offended believer has **no** effect on what God will do. God is true to Himself.

He will judge righteously whether or not an offended believer obeys him in using vertical forgiveness.

It is not God who is affected by vertical forgiveness. It is the offended believer. By means of prayer and as an act of the will, an offended believer releases to God what already belongs to God—he acknowledges that it is God's right, not his, to punish *(get even)*, and he covenants with God that he will not try to get even.

After releasing to God the penalty of an offense, an offended believer must treat his offender with *agape* love. And *agape* love may include initiating church discipline.

In like manner, if church discipline fails, or if there is a crime against society, *agape* love may require that the offended believer press civil charges or be a witness for the prosecution.

So releasing to God the penalty of an offense *(vertical forgiveness)* has **no** effect on God's judgment of the offender, church discipline, or civil government.

It is not God, nor the church, nor civil government that is affected by vertical forgiveness. It is the offended believer himself. By his obedience in releasing to God the penalty of the offense, he maintains his fellowship with God and prevents powerlessness in prayer, so that neither his progressive sanctification nor his future rewards are jeopardized (Mark 11:25; 1 Cor. 3:11-15).

Another effect of vertical forgiveness is release of the offended believer from emotional pain, bitterness, wrath, anger, and ill-will—ill-will that so often results in sinful verbal communications (Eph. 4:31-32). Vertical forgiveness "pulls the stinger" out of an offense.

While vertical forgiveness is a personal matter between a believer and his Lord, horizontal forgiveness is a personal matter between the offended person and the offender *(whether either, both, or neither are believers)*.

In horizontal forgiveness, in response to repentance *(and restitution, if appropriate)* the offended person releases the offense to the offender. Releasing the offense to the offender also releases the offender from the alienation that his offense caused.

Horizontal forgiveness has **no** effect on God's judgment of sin, and it may, or may not, have an effect on church discipline. Horizontal forgiveness granted by an offended individual does not necessarily release the local church from its obligation to discipline a member of the local congregation. Loving the offender is the guiding principle.

In the procedure of Matthew 18, church discipline is to be used only after the first two steps fail: first going alone to confront the offender, then taking one or two others. Believers are not to resort to civil government to settle grievances between them unless church discipline fails (Matt. 18:17; 1 Cor. 6:1).

Whether the offender is a believer or an unbeliever, a debt to society *(as opposed to an offense of one person against another)* cannot be canceled by horizontal forgiveness. When horizontal forgiveness is granted to an offender, he is released from the alienation his offense caused, but he is not released from culpability before the civil courts.

Three places in the Scriptures teach that when we are offended by another *(believer or unbeliever)*, we must unconditionally release to God the penalty of the offense *(vertical forgiveness)*.

We know that Mark 11:25 teaches unconditional forgiveness *(vertical forgiveness)*; because only one condition is specified—if you have anything against anyone.

The context of Ephesians 4:32 *("before the sun goes down," vs. 26, and "let all," vs. 31)* teaches that, when offended by others, our forgiveness *(vs. 32)* is to be unconditional *(vertical forgiveness)*.

In like manner, in Colossians 3:13, "If anyone has a complaint against another" teaches that, when offended by others, our forgiveness is to be unconditional *(vertical forgiveness)*.

There are remarkable similarities, not only between God's repetitive judicial forgiveness and our vertical forgiveness, but also between God's repetitive fellowship forgiveness and our horizontal forgiveness.

- In **repetitive judicial forgiveness**, God unconditionally forgives *(releases)* each believer from the penalty of each of his sins.

- In **vertical forgiveness**, believers unconditionally *(in obedience to God)* forgive *(release to God)* the penalty of each offense of their offenders.

- In **repetitive fellowship forgiveness**, God conditionally *(in response to confession of sins)* forgives *(releases)* believers from alienation of fellowship with God caused by their sins.

- In **horizontal forgiveness**, offended individuals, believers or unbelievers, conditionally *(in response to repentance)* forgive their offenders *(release them from alienation caused by their offenses)*.

Of the six kinds of forgiveness taught in the Bible, two of the four, initial judicial forgiveness and initial fellowship forgiveness are empowered by **sinners** calling on the name of the Lord through prayer (Rom. 10:13). And the other two are empowered by prayers of **believers**:

- **God's repetitive fellowship forgiveness**— empowered by praying and confessing sins.

- **Vertical forgiveness**—empowered by prayer in which the offended believer releases to God the penalty of each offense of another

Two more prayer-empowered principles were discussed:

- Prayer and confession of a personal sin *(such as pride or selfishness)* when that personal sin makes anger or hurt feelings resulting from the offense of another person disproportionately large

- Prayer for "enemies"—anyone that a believer has bad feelings toward

Thus a primary goal of this book is to teach prayer-empowered principles for overcoming the offenses of others— offenses which can be hindrances to the Christian life, offenses which God wants to use for good in the offended believer's life (Rom. 8:28-29).

The prayers of these God-empowered principles are not prayers of adoration, praise, worship, or petition, although such should be included. And they are not necessarily accompanied by feelings of "wanting to." They are motivated by obedient action—obedience to the will of God even though feelings may be screaming, "No, I don't want to!"

Believers would have greater power in prayer if they used vertical forgiveness whenever offended, thereby avoiding an out-of-fellowship condition with God.

Many Christians *(even church leaders)* would avoid falling into spiritual ditches, a multitude of marriages would be saved, many friendships would be left intact, and many church disputes would be healed and church splits avoided, if vertical forgiveness were taught and practiced.

The wisdom and insight of Lenski on forgiveness, who wrote about fifty years ago, goes beyond that of most other Bible expositors. Clearly seeing that forgiveness, not confrontation nor any other kind of communication, is the surest path for solving disputes, he comments on Ephesians 4:32:

> The Christian way of settling quarrels is the easiest thing in the world. The pastor is not to bring the two quarreling persons together in order to decide who is wronging, who is wronged— when there is perhaps guilt on both sides, what the degree of guilt is, and how it is to be apportioned. Can the pastor act the part of God and see into the hearts? No, let him go to each separately and see to it that each from the heart forgives as God has forgiven him in Christ. Let him make each face God until any grudge in his heart has disappeared. Then, and not until then, let the pastor bring them together in God's name. Then after each has in his heart forgiven the other, hands and hearts will go out, lips will confess any wrong which either or both have done, and the quarrel will be ended to stay ended.[1]

Lenski's teachings on forgiveness are worthy reminders of both the power of vertical forgiveness and the necessity of obediently using vertical forgiveness.[2]

May the power of forgiveness be effective in your life and in the lives of those whom God has put under your teaching.

Definitions— Kinds of Forgiveness

God grants four kinds of forgiveness. To forgive means to release someone from something. In all of the kinds of forgiveness that God grants, God releases man. That is, in all four, the release is downward in direction:

- **Initial Judicial Forgiveness:**
  In response to saving faith, God releases each trusting sinner from the **penalty** of **all** sins he has committed **up to** the moment of his saving faith and justification *(a one-time occurrence for each believer.)*

- **Initial Fellowship Forgiveness:**
  In response to saving faith, God **also** releases each trusting sinner from alienation of fellowship caused by sins he has committed **up to** the moment of his saving faith and justification.

- **Repetitive Judicial Forgiveness:**
  God unconditionally releases *(dependent only on His faithfulness)* each believer from the **penalty** of **each** sin he commits **after** the moment of his saving faith and justification *(upon the occasion of each sin).*

- **Repetitive Fellowship Forgiveness:**
  God releases each believer from alienation of
  fellowship caused by sins he commits after his
  saving faith and justification, in response to his
  obedience in both confession of his personal sins
  and in using vertical forgiveness *(unconditionally
  releasing to God the penalty of each offense of
  another against himself)*.

In addition to the four kinds of forgiveness that God
grants, the Scriptures teach two more kinds of forgiveness. Believers are to obey God by using both kinds:

- **Vertical Forgiveness:**
  God commands each believer to pray and unconditionally release to Him the **penalty** of each offense of another person *(believer or unbeliever)*
  against him *(the offended believer)* **whenever** he
  is offended by **anyone** *(even if the offender never
  repents)*.

- **Horizontal Forgiveness**:
  In response to repentance by an offender *(unless
  present performance, such as refusal to make
  restitution, denies the reality of his repentance)*,
  God commands the offended person to forgive.
  That is, he is to release the offense to his offender,
  thereby also releasing the offender from alienation
  caused by his offense.

Explanatory Comments:

Vertical forgiveness *(releasing to God the penalty
of an offense)* is an act of the will, not feelings. It is a
commitment—a **binding verbal contract** with God,
made by prayer, in which the offended believer releases
to God his *(the offended believer's)* supposed right to get
even. In this act of obedience to his Lord, the offended

believer **acknowledges** that it is God, not himself, who has the right to vengeance; and he **pledges** that he will not pursue vindictiveness.

Vertical forgiveness *(releasing the penalty of an offense to God)* has **no** effect on God's future judgment and/or punishment of the offender. It is the offended believer, not God, that vertical forgiveness changes. It pulls the stinger out of the offense, taking away the offended believer's pain.

Having disarmed himself through the act of vertical forgiveness *(releasing to God the penalty of the offense)*, the offended believer can treat his offender only in ways that are consistent with *agape* love.

Since vertical forgiveness releases the penalty of the offense *(rather than releasing the offense and/or the offender)* both the offender and his offense remain unforgiven *(by the person he has offended)* **until** the offender repents *(making restitution, if appropriate)* and the offended person grants horizontal forgiveness.

Granting horizontal forgiveness to a repentant offender releases him from the alienation caused by his offense. But it does not necessarily establish a friendship that was nonexistent prior to the offense.

Granting horizontal forgiveness may, or may not, restore fellowship to the level that existed prior to the offense. And it may, but sometimes cannot, restore trust to the level that existed prior to the offense, or restore the forgiven offender to a previously-held position.

Neither vertical forgiveness *(releasing to God the penalty of an offense)* nor horizontal forgiveness *(granting forgiveness to an offender in response to his repentance)* causes amnesia. "Forgive and forget" is a fantasy that leads to disappointment and frustration.

Neither vertical forgiveness *(releasing to God the penalty of an offense)* nor horizontal forgiveness *(granting forgiveness to the offender in response to his repentance)* requires "acting as if the offense has been forgotten"; and neither means that the offended person must "never mention it again."

Neither vertical forgiveness *(releasing to God the penalty of an offense)* **nor** horizontal forgiveness *(granting forgiveness to an offender in response to his repentance)* precludes requiring repayment of a debt or making restitution **unless** one or both are specifically released by the offended person as he grants horizontal forgiveness.

Neither vertical forgiveness **nor** horizontal forgiveness releases the offender from any debt or obligation to a person other than the one who has forgiven.

Neither vertical forgiveness nor horizontal forgiveness precludes church discipline; and neither precludes **any** act of *agape* love *(however painful it might be for the offender)*.

Misunderstood— or Twisted and Mangled?

Nearly every teaching of the Scriptures has been misunderstood at some time in history. The cults are a continuing witness that many crucial biblical truths are misunderstood, or perhaps even intentionally twisted and mangled. God's teachings on forgiveness are no exception: His truth about forgiveness has been misunderstood even by some who desire above all to honor and obey God.

Errors about forgiveness are taught mouth-to-mouth and house-to-house like old wives' tales. Sooner or later they are accepted and spread as "infallible truth" by well-meaning but theologically untrained Christians, without a second thought being given to testing their veracity.

One of the most grievous errors— the one that is blasphemous— is the idea that man must forgive God. We should not be too hard, however, on the theologically untrained who teach this mistaken idea. Ordinarily those who teach this are trying to help others cope with the hurts in their lives— hurts that the Sovereign God could have prevented. But for our good and for His glory, He whose ways are higher than ours allowed each painful situation (Isa. 43:7, 55:9; Rom. 8:28-30). He who knows when a sparrow falls is with us in these painful trials (Matt. 10:29).

At times of distress, the thing the hurting believer needs most is to be close to God and to have the comfort that only He can give. But consider this: what could a hurting Christian do to harm his fellowship with God more than to attribute evil to the holy God who has never sinned and never will?

And yet that is what some well-meaning people are telling others to do. They are urging others to blame God for their troubles and then forgive Him. No, they don't actually say, "Blame God and then forgive Him." But in effect they are teaching others to charge God with sin when they teach them to "forgive God." If this concept did not include blaming God for sinful actions, then there would be no reason to forgive Him.

A second idea similar to the one just discussed is equally erroneous. It goes something like this: "We know that God isn't really guilty of any evil, but surely He wouldn't mind if we blame Him and then forgive Him, if it will make us feel better."

What a pathetically mistaken idea! Should it make a Christian feel better to blaspheme God? Rather than "forgiving" God, wouldn't it be more appropriate to pray and confess the blasphemy of even seriously contemplating such a horrible sin?

The book of Hebrews lists heroes of the faith who, because of conscience toward God, became martyrs. And through the centuries Christians have been martyred because they would not deny their faith in Christ. And yet if we look carefully, this "blame God with your fingers crossed" idea suggests: "Surely God wouldn't mind if we blasphemed Him in order that we might feel better."

Anyone who might be even slightly tempted to succumb to either of these two "forgive God" teachings should read what the Apostle Peter says about suffering: "For what credit is it if, when you are beaten for your faults, you take it patiently? But when you do good and suffer, if you take it patiently, this is commendable before God. For to this you were called, because Christ also suffered for us, leaving us an example, that you should follow His steps" (1 Pet. 2:20-21).

Obviously, no one found either the "blame God" or the "forgive Him" teaching in the Scriptures. These erroneous ideas must have come instead from the world and the "happiness doctrine" that the world promotes. In contrast to blaspheming God in a vain attempt to find peace and happiness, Jesus gives peace and joy to those who obey Him in righteousness (Rom. 14:17).

A third false teaching— one which was thoroughly discussed in chapter thirteen— is expressed in the statement, "I can't forgive myself." Even though this error is widely accepted, even among Christians, there is one primary problem with it— nowhere in the Bible is it taught.

Isn't it strange? Commonly held "truths" *(errors)* are taught as being essential to Christian life and growth, and yet God has not revealed them in His Word. Are Christians implying that God did not know the principles we need, or that He knew but didn't love us enough to put them in His Word?

Of course there are times of remorse. There are times when a Christian will regret his sinful actions of the past, and he should. There may be times when he awakens and thinks, "Surely it must be a bad dream— it can't be true. I wouldn't have done such a despicable thing. How can I ever forgive myself?" But as shown in chapter thirteen, sin is against God, not oneself. Forgiving one-self is not the answer.

A fourth erroneous teaching, although taught by learned and godly Bible teachers, is also serious. In this teaching, a creative *(but unbiblical)* method is provided for "forgiving" those who are not present. As such, this method supplants God-given power— the power of vertical forgiveness of the penalties of offenses— with a man-made "fizzle."

In this fourth erroneous teaching, Christians are instructed to sit in one chair with another chair facing them. They are to imagine that an offender is sitting in the empty chair. Then they are to vent all of their pent-up bitterness, anger, and wrath against the offender— a person who is absent and who may even be dead. After spewing out verbal venom, they are to tell that imaginary person that they forgive him.

What if the offender were really sitting in the chair? Would he be edified *(built up)*? What would he say? The Scriptures teach that the offended should confront his offender— speaking the truth in love for the purpose of helping restore the offender to fellowship with God, with himself, and with other believers. He should not attempt to help himself feel better by spewing out venomous words, even if he is alone (Matt. 12:36, 18:15-17; Gal. 6:1; Eph. 4:15, 4:29).

To teach or encourage believers to confront an offender, even an imagined person, with anything but *agape* love is contrary to biblical teaching. Rather than being biblical, it is secular. According to secular "truth" *(error)*, one way to handle problems is to "ventilate" feelings by using hateful words or violent actions.

God gives simple instructions that yield powerful results— much more powerful than talking to an empty chair; much more powerful than talking to an imaginary person, whether dead or alive; and without sinful words and actions. God says, "Turn offenses over to Me, and I will take care of them" (Mark 11:25; Rom. 12:19), paraphrased).

And yet some believers, even godly Christians, have misunderstood and replaced God's truth with a farce in which Christians talk to imaginary persons about their problems— even a person who may be dead— instead of talking to the living God!

In a fifth erroneous concept, the offended person writes the offenses against him on a piece of paper and then destroys the paper. In some mystical manner, by symbolizing forgiveness, he supposedly forgives the offense.

If a believer has accepted this erroneous idea of writing offenses down on paper and then symbolically destroying the paper, should we expect his attempts to forgive to be much more than a "fizzle?"

Can we do anything less than reject the "imaginary person in the chair" forgiveness and "symbolic paper" forgiveness as being contrary to biblical teaching and therefore lacking God's power?

If we teach unbelievers ways to feel better without a personal relationship with Christ, are we really helping them? Haven't we failed them at their point of greatest need?

If we teach believers how to find some relief from bitterness, wrath, and anger without teaching them how to find renewed fellowship with God as well as relief from bad feelings by using vertical forgiveness, are we really helping them?

Misunderstood— or twisted and mangled? Try as we might, with the limitation of human understanding, we are unable to understand the depths of God's Word with complete accuracy. Not being able to understand His Word flawlessly, we are always in danger of misrepresenting a portion of His truth. Who is there among us who can't remember something that we once taught as biblical truth but have replaced now that we have a more carefully developed understanding?

May each of us, therefore, be diligent in searching the Scriptures daily to evaluate everything we hear or read in the light of the Scriptures so that we may broaden our understanding of the Scriptures, reject error, teach biblical truth with understanding and clarity, and edify the saints—all to the glory of God.

Sexual Relations After Adultery?

What about sexual relations? Must they be resumed after adultery? If so, when? Before the offender "turns" and says he repents? After he "turns" and says he repents? Under what conditions? These are difficult questions, especially now with the increase in the incidence, variety, and severity of sexually-transmitted diseases. In order to simplify our discussion, it will be assumed that the husband is the adulterer, but most of the biblical principles apply equally when the wife is an adulteress.

Some basic biblical principles are:

- Loving God with *agape* love means obeying Him.

- In obedience to God, an offended wife must pray and unconditionally release the penalty of her husband's offenses against her to her Lord.

- She must love her husband with *agape* love, no matter how she feels, even if she despises him and feels that he is her enemy.

- God says that a wife must meet her husband's sexual needs (1 Cor. 7:5 with Matt. 22:37, John 14:15, Mark 11:25, and Luke 6:27-28).

Let's reconsider some implications of these biblical principles. The offended wife cannot do anything out of spite or out of desire for personal vengeance. She cannot attempt to get even. Although her feelings of being betrayed and/or "being used" seem overwhelming, her feelings are not a sufficient reason to withhold sexual relations.

Loving her husband with *agape* love means doing things purposefully for his good, without regard to her feelings. Even though her feelings may scream that she is being used, she cannot be used if she has sexual relations with her husband to please God. Instead, she is serving the Lord Christ (1 Cor. 7:3-5; Col. 3:23-24). She may be surprised, as she wholeheartedly serves her Lord by loving her husband with *agape* love, that her attitude toward her adulterous husband becomes one of sorrow for him.

And if, in addition to loving her husband with agape love, she thinks of her husband standing either at the great white throne judgment or at the judgment seat of Christ, how can her anger over his betrayal of her and their marriage vows be greater than her sorrow for him (2 Cor. 5:10; Rev. 20:11-12)?

The biblical validity of the discussion thus far does not depend upon the adulterer's supposed repentance. It depends instead only upon the law of love. However, let's consider what the adulterous mate's attitude should be.

If he has really repented of his adultery, will he want to take any chance of infecting his wife with a sexually-transmitted disease? If he has really repented, won't he want to be tested for sexually-transmitted diseases?

If he has really repented, won't he decide to abstain from sexual relations, or at the very least, decide to adhere to sexual practices that are the least likely to transmit HIV *(the virus responsible for AIDS)* to her until such time as tests will show whether or not he has contracted the disease? How could any husband say he had repented if he were not concerned that his sin bring on his wife the uncertainty or anguish of acquiring a sexually-transmitted disease and possibly facing an untimely death?

Regarding sexual relations that are "least likely" to transmit HIV, according to some authorities, so-called safe sex is so risky that becoming infected is only a matter of time. If these authorities are correct, so-called safe sex might be likened to playing Russian roulette. The bullet may not be in the top chamber the first time the trigger is pulled, but it won't be long until tragedy strikes.

Obtain reliable medical advice. For instance, what is the usual length of time until tests can determine if a person carries the HIV? How much can this time vary, and how likely is it that the time will extend beyond the usual time? How can a person who is infected best protect the uninfected? Is kissing dangerous?

It has been reported that mothers infected with AIDS transmit it to the babies they bear. Whether other children in the family, other than nursing babies, are in danger of contracting the disease in nonsexual contacts is a question to be answered by authorities on the subject.

But there are differences among authorities. To those of us who are not physicians, it is difficult to choose one to follow. However, among books worthy of study is: *AIDS: The Unnecessary Epidemic*, Stanley Monteith, M.D., published by Covenant House Books, P.O. Box 4690, Sevierville, Tennessee 37864.

Also worthy of study is: *AIDS: What the Government Isn't Telling You*, Lorraine Day, M.D., published by Rockford Press, 44-489 Town Center Way, Suite D-412, Palm Desert, California 92260.

If a husband does not have sufficient concern for his wife's health to protect her from a sexually-transmitted disease after he has supposedly repented of his adulterous behavior, his attitude/actions **contradict** his alleged repentance. She should **not** grant horizontal forgiveness to him.

But what about resuming sexual relations after adultery? Let's consider some biblical principles:

- The wife is to submit to her husband in everything (Eph. 5:22-24).

- They each have authority over the body of the other (1 Cor. 7:4).

- Neither is to defraud the other sexually (1 Cor. 7:5).

- The husband and wife have become one flesh (Eph. 5:31).

- An adulterous mate has become one flesh with another person (1 Cor. 6:15-16).

- When there is adultery, sexual relations in that marriage have not fulfilled one of God's purposes for sexual relations in marriage: to prevent sexual sin (1 Cor. 7:5).

Let's consider God's plan for marriage partners to help their mates avoid falling into sexual sin. What if a wife has been sexually defrauding her husband, and in response, he has become involved in adultery? Who then is responsible for his adultery? The wife? Or the husband? He is. In obedience to God, he is to love his wife with *agape* love no matter how she behaves

(Eph. 5:25). He is guilty, no matter how often or how long she sexually defrauded him.

However, if she has sexually defrauded him, she has sinned by defying God (1 Cor. 7:3-5). She needs to confess her sin to God and ask her husband's forgiveness. Even though he is guilty of adultery, she has sinned against her husband, and she needs to ask his forgiveness. But her sin of sexually defrauding him in no way excuses his sin of adultery.

Both need to get right with God by confessing their own sins, and they both need to get right with each other by asking for and granting forgiveness. Both are one hundred percent guilty, but they are guilty of different sins.

Now let's consider some other biblical principles that apply to the offended wife:

- Her body is the temple of the Holy Spirit (1 Cor. 6:19).

- She was purchased by Jesus' death on the cross, so she does not own herself (1 Cor. 6:19).

- One of her primary obligations is to glorify God in her body (1 Cor. 6:20).

- One way of glorifying God in her body is to love God enough to obey Him, having sexual relations with her husband (John 14:15).

- Being stricken with a serious or even fatal disease and facing an untimely death, if it can be prevented, is not necessarily a way of glorifying God in her body (Matt. 5:16).

- A mother who dies of AIDS *(or another sexually-transmitted disease)* can't help her husband bring

up their children in the nurture and admonition of
the Lord (Eph. 6:4).

- Transmitting AIDS to children that God may give
  them is not an act of love.

We are considering a difficult subject, and we need
a biblically-balanced solution to the problem. After
considering the preceding verses and their implications,
I conclude:

- A husband who has committed adultery has become one flesh with another person through his
  act(s) of adultery, severing his wife from their one-
  flesh relationship while he persists in adultery,
  thereby **releasing** her from God's requirement for
  sexual relations.

- However, whether or not he "turns" and says that
  he repents, she must unconditionally forgive the
  penalty of his adultery and love him with *agape*
  love.

- Therefore, no matter how hurt she feels, and no
  matter how much she may feel used, she should
  have sexual relations with him **if** and **when** she
  can be reasonably assured that sexual relations
  will not result in either her or their children contracting a sexually-transmitted disease.

- Loving a husband who continues in adultery, or
  who repeatedly chooses to engage in adultery,
  may mean withholding sexual relations until he
  consistently chooses his wife to be one flesh with
  him.

- And loving a husband who continues in adultery
  may mean bringing the influence of the church to
  bear upon her husband, through counseling and/or
  church discipline.

If the adulterous husband does not follow through with counseling and godly changes, the local church should be faithful in its love for the husband, the wife, the children, the membership of the local church, and a watching world. The local church must exercise church discipline in an all-out effort to restore the adulterous husband to fellowship with God, with his wife, and with the local church.

Many marriages would be saved from calamities such as adultery and divorce if others really cared, loving wisely:

- Neither taking sides nor supporting sinful actions or reactions

- Neither participating in nor encouraging gossip or slander

- Not diverting a troubled marriage partner from seeking real help until it is too late to save the marriage by "being a good listener"

- But instead, seeking to lead couples in troubled marriages to real help through biblical counseling

Preferably, both husband and wife should obtain counseling. But, loving wisely also includes an understanding that God often works first, or even exclusively, through only one marriage partner (1 Pet. 3:1).

The one whose desire is to please God should be encouraged to seek biblical counseling. God's will for that one is to have peace and joy while being conformed into the image of His Son (John 14:27; Rom. 8:28-29; Col. 1:11).

Notes

Chapter One—Power, Puzzles, and Fizzles

1. Since this book pertains to forgiveness, and since God's forgiveness of sin can best be understood by the doctrine of justification, much of our study in chapters one and two will be focused on the doctrine of justification. Therefore, in most instances, to distinguish the moment of saving faith and justification from time subsequent to justification, we will use such terminology as "the moment of justification," and "subsequent to justification."

2. From the Greek verb λογίζομαι *(logizomai)* "to place to someone's account." William F. Arndt and F. Wilbur Gingrich, *A Greek-English Lexicon of the New Testament and Other Early Christian Literature* (4th rev. and augmented ed., Chicago: The University of Chicago Press, 1952, hereinafter referred to as BAG), 476-77.

3. Forms of the verb ἀφίημι *(aphiēmi)* are used for God's forgiveness of man (e.g., Matt. 6:12-15; Mark 11:25; Luke 5:21; 1 John 1:9). Forms of this same verb are used for man's forgiveness of man (e.g., Matt. 6:12-15; Mark 11:25; Luke 17:3-4). Forms of the verb χαρίζομαι *(charizomai)* are used of God's forgiveness of man, and/or man's forgiveness of man (e.g., Luke 7:43; 2 Cor. 2:10; Eph. 4:32; Col. 2:13, 3:13).

4. Lexical meanings of ἀφίημι *(aphiēmi)* include "let go," "cancel," "remit," and "pardon." Χαρίζομαι *(charizomai)* includes similar meanings: "remit," "forgive," and "pardon." Thus, it can be seen that "to release," as used in this book, is a basic equivalent of the various lexical meanings listed here. BAG, 124-25, 884-85.

5. Again with regard to ἀφίημι *(aphiēmi)*, secular meanings of this verb in early Greek included: "to send off," "release," and "to release someone from a legal relation." New Testament meanings include "to let go," "to remit," and "to forgive." *Theological Dictionary of the New Testament*, vol. 1, 509.

6. With regard to χαρίζομαι *(charizomai)*, in the New Testament a basic meaning is "to give" (TDNT, vol. 9, 396). Twice in the New Testament this verb is used "in a legal sense for showing favour in a trial, though in directly opposite ways. Thus Barabbas is 'given' *[released]* to the people . . . but Paul is 'given up' *[released]* to the Jews . . . ." Again, it can be seen that "to release" is an accurate translation of both ἀφίημι *(aphiēme)* and χαρίζομαι *(charizomai)*. TDNT, vol. 9, 393.

7. Charles C. Ryrie, *Basic Theology* (Wheaton, IL: Victor Books, 1986), 292.

8. In *Forgiveness: The Power and the Puzzles*, the discussion of reconciliation is limited to those aspects that are germane to our discussion of forgiveness. For a more complete discussion, yet one that is concise, see Ryrie, *Basic Theology*, 292-97.

9. Pastor David E. Childs, Twin Branch Bible Church, Mishawaka, Indiana.

10. Reference to 1 John 5:7 has been omitted since this witness to the Trinity is not included in the critical texts, such as the United Bible Societies' text, and has no support in the majority text except for the *Textus Receptus.*

11. TDNT, vol. 1, 255.

12. One of God's requirements for continued fellowship of the believer with Himself is taught in the first chapter of John's first epistle. For an insightful and helpful study of 1 John 1:5-10, see Zane Hodges, "Fellowship and Confession," *Bibliotheca Sacra* 129 (1972): 48-60.

Chapter Two—What About Believers' Sins?

1. Philip Schaff, *History of the Christian Church* (n.p.: Charles Scribner's Sons, 1910; reprint ed., Grand Rapids: Wm. B. Eerdmans Publishing Company, 1967), vol. 2, *Ante-Nicene Christianity*, 254.

2. It might seem more natural to speak of sins committed after "regeneration" than after "justification." However, this book deals with forgiveness, and forgiveness is more clearly seen from the standpoint of justification.

3. "Priest" is not in the Greek text of Hebrews 10:12, nor is the word "man." By context (vs. 11), the "man" of Hebrews 10:12 is a priest; and by considering His superior Priesthood, we know that Jesus Christ (vs. 10) is our High Priest. In like manner, "priest" is not in the Greek text of Hebrews 7:24, nor is "man." However, both "priest" and "high priest" are in the immediate context (vss. 23 and 26).

4. Walter A. Elwell, gen. ed., *Baker Encyclopedia of the Bible*, 2 vols. (Grand Rapids: Baker Book House, 1988 ed.), vol. 2, 1614.

5. In addition to these lexical meanings, Arndt and Gingrich state that Latin translators of the New Testament have commonly rendered παράκλητος *(paraklētos)* as *advocatus*. BAG, 623.

6. In Romans 10:9-10 "confession" is taught as it pertains to confessing Jesus Christ as Savior at the moment of saving faith and justification. In stark contrast, the "confession" of 1 John 1:9 pertains to confessing personal sins. Confessing Jesus—the only one who is holy—and confessing personal sins should not be confused.

Chapter Three—If We Will, He Will

1. While the King James Version and the New King James Version both translate Matthew 6:12 "as we forgive," other versions translate "as we have forgiven." The differences in translations correctly reflect variations in the Greek manuscripts. However, the meaning is not changed. Translated either way, the teaching is that God's forgiveness of believers is dependent upon their forgiveness of others.

2. Richard C. H. Lenski, although he wrote about a half century ago, still provides some of the most insightful comments on verses dealing with forgiveness. Lenski says:

   > It is most vital for acceptable prayer that the petitioner forgive all his fellow men. Let us not delude ourselves that we are most firmly believing and filling our prayers with faith while secretly, in our hearts, we hold something against somebody.

   R. C. H. Lenski, *The Interpretation of St. Mark's Gospel* (n.p.: The Wartburg Press, 1946; reprint ed., Minneapolis: Augsburg Publishing House, 1964), 496.

3. The problem of believing and accepting alleged repentance of an offender who has repeatedly offended you and who has repeatedly returned to you to ask for forgiveness (Luke 17:4) will be considered in chapter seven. Also in chapter seven, the relationship between actions and the words "turn" and "saying" of Luke 17:4 will be discussed.

4. The critical text of the United Bible Societies does not even indicate a variant reading that says "forgive **him**."

5. Zane C. Hodges and Arthur L. Farstad, editors of *The Greek New Testament According to the Majority Text* (Nashville: Thomas Nelson Publishers, 1982), provide additional evidence that the word "him" is not translated from any textual evidence, but merely reflects a word that has been inserted by translators with the intent of clarifying the passage.

6. Mark 11:26, as translated by the New King James Version, reads: "But if you do not forgive, neither will your Father in heaven forgive your trespasses." And the King James Version translates: "But if ye do not forgive, neither will your Father which is in heaven forgive your trespasses." Notice that both translations read: "If you do not forgive," not "If you do not forgive **him**."

   Verse 26 is omitted from several versions, such as the American Standard Version, the Revised Standard Version, the New American Standard Version, and the New International Version that follow critical texts, such as the United Bible Societies' text.

Even though verse 26 has been omitted from the critical text, it has a strong witness in the majority text, and Codex Ephraemi Rescriptus (C) sides with the majority text. Hodges and Farstad, *Majority Text.*

All four of the above-mentioned translations *(that follow the critical text)* include verse 26 in marginal readings. It is interesting to notice that none of the four add **him** after forgive. And yet, all four erroneously add **him** to verse 25.

7. See Notes 3-6 of chapter one.

8. "Thought" is used here as a volitional activity in which the offended person relishes vindictive thoughts. "Ventilating feelings" during "adult" temper tantrums by beating a pillow, which is typical secular advice, may include vindictive thoughts.

9. Commenting on Jesus' command to forgive in Mark 11:25, Lenski asks the rhetorical question: "When?" Again he queries: "After the person admits our charge, confesses it, and asks remission?" He answers: "The Scriptures fix no such time. The remission is to take place at once, the moment we feel aggrieved against anyone." Lenski, *Mark*, 497.

10. Although Lenski fails to provide a complete and well-balanced view on forgiveness, he does realize that forgiveness through prayer does **not** preclude either confrontation or church discipline. In his commentary on Ephesians 4:32 Lenski says:

> Let us put this plainly since even pastors misunderstand it. The moment a man wrongs me I must forgive him. Then my soul is free. If I hold the wrong against him I sin against God and against him and jeopardize my forgiveness with God. Whether the man repents, makes amends, asks my pardon or not, makes no difference. I have instantly forgiven him. He must face God with the wrong he has done; but that is his affair and God's and not mine save that in the case he is a brother I should help him according to Matt. 18:15, etc. But whether this succeeds or not and before this even begins I must forgive him.

R. C. H. Lenski, *The Interpretation of St. Paul's Epistles to the Galatians, to the Ephesians, and to the Philippians* (Lutheran Book Concern, 1937; reprint ed., Minneapolis: Augsburg Publishing House, 1961), 588.

11. Since Luke 17:3 teaches that the offender *(the person)* must be forgiven *(released)* when he repents, he cannot be forgiven **before** he repents. Since this is true, it might be thought that the offense *(act)* is forgiven in the vertical forgiveness of Mark 11:25. However, if the forgiveness of Mark 11:25 actually did release the offense, no offense

would remain, and it would be impossible to rebuke the offender for his offense, as required in Luke 17:3.

The Scriptures confirm the logic that vertical forgiveness does **not** release the offense. In Matthew 6:14, trespasses are released to the offender, not to God. Notice the use of the dative and genitive cases in the Greek text of Matthew 6:14: ". . . ἀφῆτε τοῖς ἀνθρώποις τὰ παραπτώματα αὐτῶν . . ."

To take the position that Mark 11:25 teaches forgiving the offense *(act)* results in the same problem as assuming that this verse teaches forgiving the offender *(the person)*. As some Bible scholars have recognized, if it is the offender that is forgiven in Mark 11:25, then how can he be confronted later? And how can he again be granted forgiveness when he repents, as required in Luke 17:3? In like manner, if it is the offense that is forgiven in Mark 11:25, on what basis can the offender be confronted later?

With either of these two erroneous assumptions about the forgiveness of Mark 11:25 *(offender forgiven, offense forgiven)*, there is a problem. It is impossible to use the rebuking and forgiving of Luke 17:3, the confronting of Matthew 18:15-16, and/or the church discipline of Matthew 18:17.

Again, we see that our forgiveness of others and their offenses is to be strikingly similar to God's forgiveness of us. God grants us repetitive judicial forgiveness unconditionally, and He grants us repetitive fellowship forgiveness dependent upon confession. In like manner, we are to unconditionally release to God the **penalty** that we might want to inflict on those who offend us, and we are to grant our offenders horizontal forgiveness when *(the condition and the time)* they repent.

12. As discussed in Note 6, the New King James Version translates Mark 11:26: "But if you do not forgive, neither will your Father in heaven forgive you your trespasses"; and the King James Version translates: "But if ye do not forgive, neither will your Father which is in heaven forgive you your trespasses."

Thus, Mark 11:26 is in agreement with Mark 11:25: neither verse says that we are to forgive **him**—the offender. Instead, both teach that God will not forgive our trespasses unless we use vertical forgiveness, releasing to God the penalty of the offense.

Whether this agreement of Mark 11:26 with verse 25 is considered significant to the reader will depend upon: (1) his overall view of the critical text vs. the majority text; and/or (2) his evaluation of the manuscript evidence without particular adherence to either textual tradition.

Chapter Four—Forgive and What?

1. Since it is so commonly thought that God forgets sins, it would seem
    that the subject of forgetting would be more commonly included in
    theological writings, either in conjunction with teaching on forgiveness
    or separately. However, many theological works, both scholarly and
    popular, ignore this subject.

    For instance, "forget" is not included as a subject heading in *The
    New International Dictionary of the New Testament*, edited by
    Colin Brown, 3 volumes (Grand Rapids: Zondervan, 1975-1978),
    and no reference to forgetting is included in the six page discussion
    of "forgiveness." However, in volume 2, page 366, under the subject
    of "judgment," the writer says, "Before God nothing is forgotten,
    whether deed or word."

2. *The Baker Encyclopedia*, 1988 ed., (vol. 1, 811) includes a full page
    discussion about forgiveness, covering both God's forgiveness of man,
    and man's forgiveness of man, but no section of this two volume set
    is set apart to discuss the subject of forgetting, and no statement re-
    garding forgetting is included in the section on forgiveness.

3. In the New Testament, "forget" is translated from ἐπιλανθάνομαι
    (epilanthanomai) more often than from any other Greek word (Matt.
    16:5; Mark 8:14; Luke 12:6; Phil. 3:13; Heb. 6:10, 13:16; James
    1:24). In addition to literal meanings, this Greek word includes such
    nonliteral meanings as "neglect, overlook, care nothing about." BAG,
    295.

4. It would be interesting, and no doubt helpful, to study the meanings of
    the Hebrew words from which "forget" is translated in the Old Testa-
    ment. However, even though we are not studying the meanings of any
    individual Hebrew words in this book, we are studying the ways in
    which the Holy Spirit has used Hebrew words in the Old Testament
    to convey the biblical concepts of "forgetting." While this contextual
    study would seem to be adequate for this book, some may want to
    study "forgetting" in more depth.

5. Speaking of both שָׁכַח *(shakach)* and ἐπιλανθάνομαι *(epilanthano-
    mai)*, *The International Standard Bible Encyclopaedia* says:

    > "Forget" is to fail to hold in mind, and the forgetfulness may be
    > either innocent or blameworthy . . . It is also used in the sense of
    > God forgetting or seeming not to care . . . "To forget" sometimes
    > means to forsake . . .

    The International Standard Bible Encyclopaedia, James Orr, Gen-
    eral Editor, 5 vols. (Grand Rapids: Eerdmans, 1929; reprint ed.,
    Wilmington: Associated Publishers and Authors, n.d.), vol. 2, 1132.

Chapter Five—Why Forgive?

1. In the preceding context, Peter had asked about forgiveness (Matt. 18:21). It is likely that Peter was thinking of horizontal forgiveness— forgiveness in which the offender repents *(or says that he repents)* and asks for forgiveness. One reason to think that Jesus was speaking of horizontal forgiveness is because Jesus had taught about confrontation *(for the purpose of restoring an offending brother)* earlier in the chapter (Matt. 18:15-18).

    Another reason for thinking that Peter was thinking of horizontal forgiveness is that the Greek text says, "Forgive **him**" (Matt. 18:21). If so, then inclusion of "him" in the text accurately reflects Peter's question.

    However, even though the preceding context teaches horizontal forgiveness—forgiveness that is granted in response to repentance— it does not necessarily mean that the text which follows is also teaching horizontal forgiveness. It is not unusual for Jesus to start with a known teaching and then proceed to teach a new and deeper principle. For instance, He starts by repeating the Old Testament prohibition against adultery, and then He introduces a new principle —adultery in the heart (Matt. 5:27-28).

    Therefore, even though the earlier subject is horizontal forgiveness, there is no persuasive reason to believe that Jesus continues to talk of horizontal forgiveness in His illustration of Matthew 18:23-35. Instead, we can let the text speak for itself, and its teaching pictures vertical forgiveness.

2. When we read in Matthew 18:35 that our forgiveness of others must be "from the heart," we should consider why Jesus includes these three words.

    In the New Testament, *heart* "more frequently denotes the seat of intellectual and spiritual life, the inner life in opposition to external appearance." NIDNT, vol. 2, 182.

    Therefore, whether we grant **horizontal** forgiveness verbally in response to the request of a person who says he repents, or whether we forgive the penalty of the offenses of others unconditionally by means of **vertical** forgiveness, for our forgiveness to be acceptable to God, it must be "from the heart" (Matt. 18:35; Mark 11:25; Luke 17:3).

3. The King James Version includes the words, "their trespasses," and the New King James Version includes the words, "his trespasses," whereas some other versions omit any reference to "trespasses" (Matt. 18:35). Critical texts of the Greek New Testament, such as the United

Bible Societies' text and Nestle's Greek New Testament, leave out "his trespasses."

4. The authenticity of the words "his trespasses" in Matthew 18:35 is attested to by a strong witness in the majority text, and by the inclusion, along with these Western texts, of Codex Ephraemi Rescriptus (C). Even though Codex Sinaiticus (ℵ) and Codex Alexandrinus (B) omit "his trespasses," there is not a consensus among the Egyptian texts for omitting "his trespasses," since (C) sides with the majority text. Hodges and Farstad, editors, *Majority Text.*

5. Variations from the critical text as reproduced in the majority text and their relationship to our understanding of forgiveness are interesting and worthy of additional study.

Chapter Six—I Don't Feel Like It!

1. *Agape* love has been defined in this chapter as purposeful dedication to the good of another person as it relates to an offender. Since there is considerable disagreement as to the differences in meaning between ἀγαπάω *(agapaō)* and φιλέω *(phileō)*, it is appropriate to consider the meanings of both words.

2. TDNT devotes 34 pages to the study of ἀγαπάω *(agapaō)* in volume 1 and 33 pages to the study of φιλέω *(phileō)* in volume 9. After studying ἀγαπάω *(agapaō)* as it relates to Old Testament teaching, teaching in the Septuagint, teaching in various parts of the New Testament, and the Post-Apostolic Period, near the end of the study it says: "There grows up a Church which knows of a love that does not desire but gives." TDNT, vol. 1, 55.

3. In accordance with TDNT, some say that *agape* love is giving. God is *agape* love, and yet, among other things, He is a God who sometimes withholds, giving only what is good, even as loving parents withhold from a child all the candy he wants (2 Cor. 12:7-10). Therefore, the definition "*agape* love is giving" is both inadequate and erroneous.

4. Some say that *agape* love is God's kind of love, and *philia* love is man's kind of love. However, these definitions both fail under even superficial scrutiny. In 1 John 2:15, *agape* is used twice for love that is sinful, and this certainly is not "God's kind of love." And *philia* is used to express love that God the Father has for God the Son (John 5:20). No one would dare to suggest that the love that the Father has for the Son is inferior or "man's kind of love."

5. A simple word study of the use of ἀγαπάω *(agapaō)* and φιλέω *(phileō)* in the New Testament yields definitions that are more satisfying to the author than the ones given above. In this word study, all of

the uses of both of these Greek words in the New Testament are divided into three groups, in accordance with how each use is understood by context:

- Love is a feeling, whether godly or sinful.
- Love pertains to an act of the will, or to an action contrary to feelings.
- There is insufficient context to determine whether a feeling or an act of the will is meant.

As we consider these three categories, we see that various uses of ἀγαπάω *(agapaō)* are found in the category of "an act of the will, or an action contrary to feeling." With this fact in mind, we consider two additional facts about uses of ἀγαπάω *(agapaō)*. One is that ἀγαπάω *(agapaō)* is used for God's love, and the other is that this same word is used of love that is sinful (John 3:16; 1 John 2:15-16). We arrive at the conclusion that a general definition for *agape* love is: an act of the will, a dedication to someone or something, whether godly or sinful.

Realizing that, as used in the New Testament, there is no moral content in *agape (used for both godly love and sinful love)*, and realizing also that moral content is implicit in any use of ἀγαπάω *(agapaō)* that pertains to either God's love or love that He commands, we arrive at a good-sense definition for *agape* love:

> *Agape* love is an act of the will, to purpose and to do that which is best for the other person, without the necessity of emotional motivation.

That is, as God uses *agape* in the New Testament, it does not pertain to a desire *(feeling)* but to volitional acts—even when these acts of the will are contrary to feelings.

6. Feelings are God-given. Even as feelings of guilt are often used by God to bring about biblical actions, such as confession of sin, anger is a God-given indicator, revealing a problem. While living the Christian life should be characterized by believing God's Word, trusting God, and obeying Him, feelings should be understood and accepted for what they are.

Feelings are God-given indicators of a condition or a reaction to a condition. It is imperative that counselors ask counselees about their feelings—how they felt at the time of a certain occurrence and how they feel about that occurrence now. Even though time, or hardness of heart, may have dulled a counselee's feelings, to ask a counselee only for the facts, and not to be interested in knowing the feelings that attended the facts, is to dismiss God-given indicators *(feelings)* as meaningless.

7. At times, forgiveness is less than totally effective in taking away anger or bitterness toward an offender. At other times it seems that forgiveness is powerless to take away bad feelings. This problem is addressed in the chapter "When Forgiveness 'Doesn't Work.'"

8. Many thoughtful readers immediately will think of an occasion in the Scriptures that superficially might seem to teach that we should pray and ask God to forgive those who offend us.

   Jesus prayed to the Father saying: "Father, forgive them, for they do not know what they do" (Luke 23:34). Jesus was expressing the truth of Luke 23:34b (paraphrased):

   > These soldiers have been routinely assigned the grisly task of executing the judgment of Rome on a supposed criminal. As far as the soldiers know, they have been sent out to execute three criminals.

   In His prayer, Jesus was reciting a fact already known to the Father, of course, but a fact that no mere human could have known for sure, because only God can see the heart. The soldiers were not responsible for His death.

   Jesus was not requesting judicial forgiveness for any sin of any of the soldiers. If judicial release from the penalty of their sin had been His objective, instead of asking the Father to forgive them, it is more likely that He Himself would have forgiven the soldiers (Matt. 9:2, 6). There is no other place in the New Testament that even superficially implies that Jesus ever asked the Father to forgive anyone's sins.

   In addition to His prayer accurately assessing the fact that the soldiers were not guilty of His death, His prayer also accurately portrayed His concern for those who were the agents of His suffering.

9. Those thoughtful readers who wondered about Jesus praying for His executioners likely also thought about Stephen praying for the Jews who stoned him.

   Stephen, just before he died, prayed: "Lord, do not charge them with this sin" (Acts 7:60). While Stephen's prayer showed a godly concern for his self-appointed executioners, nowhere in the Scriptures is his prayer held up as an example to follow. Nowhere in the Scriptures are we taught that we should pray and ask God to forgive an offender.

   To pray and ask God to forgive another's sins does not fit a biblical understanding of God's judicial forgiveness. As we have studied in this book, God grants initial judicial forgiveness in response to saving faith—not in response to the prayers of any other individual. And He grants repetitive judicial forgiveness to believers unconditionally—not in response to prayers of either the believing sinner or anyone else.

Chapter Seven—Warning! Deep Ditches on Both Sides!

1. The fact that Luke 17:7-9 is a continuation of Jesus' teaching in Luke 17:3-4 on horizontal forgiveness can be seen by two facts: (1) verse 7 starts with the word "and," thereby showing a continuation in thought; and (2) the conjunction δὲ *(de)* that is translated "and" in verse 7 is commonly used to show that there is a relationship between thoughts or acts that are on opposite sides of the "and." This relationship between verses 4 and 7 is more correctly shown by the use of "and" in Luke 17:7 than the adversative conjunction "but" (NKJV versus KJV and NASB).

2. Should "turn" in Luke 17:4 be understood strictly in a moral sense of repentance, rather than in a physical movement that implies repentance? Should the verb *("turn")* in the principal clause carry greater emphasis than the participle *("saying")* in the subordinate clause?

   Let's consider first the relative emphasis of the verb "ἐπιστρέψη" *(epistrepsē̄, "turn")* in the principal clause, which is the first aorist subjunctive of ἐπιστρέφω *(epistrephō̄)*, versus the present active nominative participle "λέγων" *(legōn)* in the subordinate clause. Ernest DeWitt Burton calls this use of the participle the "adverbial participle of attendant circumstances." Speaking of the use of the participle as an adverb of attendant circumstances, Burton says:

   > The term "attendant" . . . does not define the temporal relation of the participle to the verb, but the logical relation . . . [A]s respects logical relation, it is presented merely as an accompaniment of the action of the verb. It does not, e.g., define the time or the cause, or the means of the action of the principal verb, but simply prefixes or adds an associated fact or conception. It is thus often equivalent to a coordinate verb with καί.

   One of the examples that Burton gives for the use of the adverbial participle of attendant circumstances is Luke 4:15. Ernest DeWitt Burton, *Syntax of the Moods and Tenses in New Testament Greek* (Grand Rapids: Kregel Publications, 1976), 173-74.

3. The New King James Version retains the participle in the Greek text of Luke 4:15 and translates: "And He taught in their synagogues, being glorified by all." In contrast, the New International Version changes the participle to a finite verb and translates: "He taught in their synagogues, and everyone praised him."

4. H. E. Dana and Julius R. Mantey teach an adverbial use of the participle that they call the circumstantial participle in their book, *A Manual Grammar of the Greek New Testament*. From their comments,

it is clear that they are describing the same use of the participle that Burton calls the "adverbial participle of attendant circumstances."

Referring to this use of the participle, Dana and Mantey say:

> A participle may not present in a distinct way any of the above functions *[referring to adverbial uses that they described previously]*, but may merely express an attendant circumstance —an additional fact or thought which is best rendered in English by the conjunction "and" with a finite construction.

One of the examples given by Dana and Mantey is Mark 16:20. "And they went out *[finite verb]* and preached *[participle]* everywhere." H. E. Dana and Julius R. Mantey, *A Manual Grammar of the Greek New Testament* (New York: The Macmillan Company, 1955), 228.

5.   With regard to Luke 17:4, the New International Version translates: ". . . and seven times comes back to you **and says**, 'I repent,' you shall forgive him" (Luke 17:4b, emphasis added). By changing the participle "saying" to the finite verb "says," and by connecting the verbs by a coordinate conjunction, it appears that the translators of the New International Version have considered the participial clause as an adverbial of attendant circumstances.

While the author generally prefers that participles in the Greek New Testament be translated with English participles, including instances where the participle is used as an adverbial participle of attendant circumstances, it would be difficult to make a strong argument for this preference.

6.   Leaving discussion of the relationship between the primary verb and subordinate clause of Luke 17:4, let's take a superficial look at the meaning of the word that is translated "turn" or "return." As previously mentioned, "turn" is translated from an aorist subjunctive of ἐπιστρέφω *(epistrephō)*. The verb ἐπιστρέφω *(epistrephō)* has meanings such as: (1) to physically "turn" or "turn back"; (2) to "turn back" or "return" in the sense of a change of mind or a change in a course of action, for the better or the worse; and (3) to "turn" in a religious or moral sense. BAG, 301.

The general grammatical distinction is whether the verb is used transitively or intransitively. When used intransitively, the verb carries the moral or religious connotation, whereas when used transitively the verb should be understood in the physical sense. Ibid.

7.   In critical texts of the Greek New Testament, such as Nestle's text, and in the United Bible Societies' text, the words "to you" follow "turn," thereby making the verb "turn" transitive in Luke 17:4. Thus, according to our lexical understanding of the verb "turn," we should

understand this verb to be speaking of a physical turning as opposed to repentance—a moral or religious turning.

8. It is interesting, although not necessarily convincing, that there is a strong witness for omitting the words "to you" from Luke 17:4 according to Hodges and Farstad, editors, *Majority Text*. If this textual family is considered to be closest to the autographs, then ἐπιστρέψῃ *(epistrepsē)* is intransitive and conveys the idea of a moral turning, that is, repentance.

9. Let's assume that ἐπιστρέψῃ *(epistrepsē)* is transitive *(in accordance with the critical text)*, and look at the context. Since the teaching of Luke 17:3 is repentance and forgiveness, and since Luke 17:4 continues the subject of repentance and forgiveness by presenting a "what if" situation, "turn" in Luke 17:4 seems to refer to a physical movement *("turn" or "return")* that implies an inward change—a supposed repentance.

10. Conclusions: From this brief study both of the verb *("turn")* and of the relative significance of the principal and subordinate clauses, it seems to the author that: (1) translating "turn" better conveys the implied repentance of the context than "return"; and (2) retaining the participle "saying," rather than changing the participle to a conjunction and a finite verb, tends to convey a correct understanding of the superiority of implied repentance over a mere vocal profession of repentance.

11. Two definitions for *agape* love are developed in Notes 1-5 of chapter six.

12. More will be said about church discipline in the next chapter. However, three facts are: (1) church discipline is biblical; (2) church discipline is an act of love undertaken to restore, not to punish; and (3) the decision as to whether or not to use church discipline should not be the question of "What will work?" Instead, the question should be, "What is the biblical and loving thing to do?" (1 Cor. 5:1-13, 6:1-5; 2 Cor. 2:4-8; Eph. 4:15).

13. Romans 8:1; 1 Corinthians 3:11-15; Hebrews 12:6.

Chapter Eight—Love: Tough or Tender?

1. Definitions for *agape* and *philia* love are developed in Notes 1-5 of chapter six.

2. As pointed out in chapter three, the Greek New Testament does not say, "And when you stand praying forgive **him** . . ." Instead it says, "And when you stand praying forgive . . ." Addition of the word

"him" by translators is unfortunate *(the KJV avoids this error)* since it tends to obscure the teaching that the **penalty** of the offense is forgiven *(released to God)*, but the offender is not forgiven until he repents (Luke 17:3-4).

Both the offense and the offender remain unforgiven until the offender repents. That is, when the offender repents, making resti-tution if such is appropriate, the offender releases the offense to the offender, thereby also forgiving him.

3. Good legal advice is recommended as a matter of church policy. It would seem the better part of wisdom for a church to formulate its policy in accordance with legal counsel from a Christian organization specializing in legal matters affecting churches and to fully instruct the congregation about church discipline before the need for church discipline arises. One of several organizations to contact for legal advice is the Christian Legal Society, 4208 Evergreen Lane, Suite 222, Annandale, VA 22003-3264, telephone (703) 642-1070.

Chapter Nine—The "Nuts and Bolts" of Horizontal Forgiveness

1. Although it was not called "horizontal forgiveness," I am indebted to Pastor Bill Goode, Executive Director of the National Association of Nouthetic Counselors (NANC), and Bob Smith, M.D., former Executive Director of NANC, for much of my understanding of this kind of forgiveness.

Chapter Ten—Overcoming Enemy Control

1. Illustration used by Pastor Bill Goode, Executive Director, NANC *(not a verbatim quotation)*.

2. Arndt and Gindrich say that Greek verb αἴρω *(airō)* has meanings of "lift up, take up, pick up, take away or carry, carry away or remove." They also say that the verb ἀρθήτω *(arthatō)* in Ephesians 4:31 is passive (aorist passive imperative of αἴρω). BAG, 23-24.

3. The form of ἀρθήτω *(arthatō)* is that of an aorist imperative middle or passive. Frietz Rienecker, in his comments on Ephesians 4:31, says that this verb is an aorist passive imperative. Fritz Rienecker, *A Linguistic Key to the Greek New Testament*, translated with additions and revisions from the German, *Sprachlicher Schluessel zum Griechischen Neuen Testament*, ed. Cleon L. Rogers, Jr. (Grand Rapids: Zondervan Publishing House, 1980, Regency Reference Library).

4. It is interesting to notice the preponderance of active imperative verbs in Ephesians 4, and then to consider the fact that the Holy Spirit must have had a purpose for changing the form to the middle or passive voice in Ephesians 4:31.

5. Dana and Mantey, in commenting on the distinction between the middle and passive voices, say in footnote ii: "The passive arose out of the middle, and the line of demarcation between them was never absolutely fixed." Their comment shows a logical reason that the middle and passive forms can have the same form. Dana and Mantey, *Manual Grammar,* 162.

6. Dana and Mantey make comments on the middle voice that are instructive. For instance, "The middle voice is that use of the verb which describes the subject as participating in the results of the action." The sense in which the subject *(the believer)* participates in the results of the action can be seen in the discussion of Ephesians 4:32 that starts in the side-heading entitled "What Must We Do?" Ibid., 157.

7. If we were to attempt to classify the use of the middle voice in Ephesians 4:31, the "permissive middle" of Dana and Mantey would seem to come the closest. They say, "The middle may represent the agent as voluntarily yielding himself to the results of the action, or seeking to secure the results of the action in his own interest." The manner in which the believer voluntarily yields himself to the results of the action, and seeks to secure the results of the action for himself, can be seen in the discussion of Ephesians 4:32 that starts in the side-heading entitled "What Must We Do?" Ibid., 160.

8. In view of the preceding discussion, and the fact that feelings are not volitional but instead God-given indicators of a situation or one's reaction to a situation, we conclude that: (1) the verb is in the middle voice; and (2) it is reasonable to stand by the translation included in most versions, "Let all . . . be put away from you."

9. Colossians 3:8 reads: "But now you yourselves are to put off all these: anger, wrath, malice, blasphemy, filthy language out of your mouth." Whereas Ephesians 4:31 uses a form of the verb αἴρω *(airō)* that is a middle or passive imperative, as confirmed by Rienecker, Colossians 3:8 uses the active imperative ἀπόθεσθε *(apothesthe)*. Rienecker, *Linguistics Key.*

10. Superficially considered, the use of the active imperative in Colossians 3:8 seems to command a volitional change of feelings, and thereby contradicts the author's assertion that feelings are not volitional. Therefore, Colossians 3:8 might seem to void some of the author's

arguments for translating Ephesians 4:31 with the admonition, "Let all . . . be put away from you. . . ." Notice, however, that the command in Colossians 3:8 is to put things out of the mouth, not out of the heart. Colossians 3:8 is teaching volitional control of actions, not feelings. In contrast, in Ephesians 4:31, the believer is to let God put away "malice."

11. "Malice" in Ephesians 4:31 is translated from κακία *(kakia)*. Arndt and Gingrich, as the first meaning, state: "in the moral sense—a. depravity, wickedness, vice generally, as opposed to virtue." This understanding of κακία *(kakia)* emphasizes contentions by the author. Whereas Colossians 3:8 speaks of voluntary action *(not sinning with the mouth)*, Ephesians 4:31 speaks of God putting away the "malice" *(heart condition)* that causes the mouth to sin.

12. In some Greek manuscripts of the New Testament, Ephesians 4:31 and 32 are connected by δέ *(de)*. While this "and" is not included in the United Bible Societies' text, it is included in Nestle's Greek New Testament and has a strong witness, not only in the majority texts, but also in Codex Sinaiticus (‭א‬) and Codex Alexandrinus (A).

13. The conjunction δέ *(de)* is not like the "and" in "Jack and Jill went up the hill." It is not like an "and" that connects parallel subjects or objects in a sentence. Instead, although it is commonly considered an adversative conjunction, this is not its only use. In Ephesians 4:32 the Greek word δὲ *(and)* shows that a special relationship exists between thoughts. Consider the sentence, "I will go to the grocery store **and** buy groceries." There is a special relationship between "go" and "buy."

14. Arndt and Gingrich, referring to this same special relationship, include in the uses of δέ *(de)*: "relating one teaching to another," and "to insert an explanation *that is.*" BAG, 171.

15. If we paraphrase a part of Ephesians 4:31 and 32 using "that is" to translate this Greek word for "and," we read: "Let all bitterness and wrath and anger . . . be put away from you . . . **that is**, be kind and considerate by forgiving others just as God in Christ also has forgiven you." The Holy Spirit used this special "and" in verse 32 to show that a special relationship exists between verses 31 and 32. That is, the way to "let God" put away bad feelings, as taught in verse 31, is "to forgive," as taught in verse 32.

16. The Greek verb ἐχαρίσατο *(echarisato)* for God's forgiveness of us is in the aorist tense and in the indicative mood. While the aorist indicative often has been translated into English by a past tense verb, it has been known for many years that the English simple past tense does

not necessarily render the aorist indicative correctly. A. T. Robertson in *A Grammar of the Greek New Testament in the Light of Historical Research* (Reprint ed., Nashville: Broadman Press, 1934), 1380, says: "Nothing is now clearer than that the Greek aorist indicative cannot be made to square regularly with the English past."

17. Going forward in time from Robertson, Dana and Mantey in *A Manual Grammar of the Greek New Testament* (196-97), speak of one use of the aorist as "the culminative aorist." They state, "This idiom may be best translated by the English *[present]* perfect when it affects a situation present to the writer, and by the pluperfect *[past perfect]* when relatively past."

18. Although it has been more common to use the English past tense than the English present perfect *(has, hath, hast, or have, with the past participle of the main verb)* to translate the aorist indicative, use of the English present perfect to translate the aorist indicative has been relatively common in most versions of the New Testament. For instance, six popular versions of the New Testament (KJV, ASV, RSV, NASB, NIV, and NKJV) are unanimous in their use of the English present perfect tense to translate the aorist indicative middle in sixteen Bible verses (Matt. 19:20, 21:16, 26:10; Mark 10:28, 14:6; Luke 1:54, 16:11, 16:12, 18:21; John 1:18, 13:18; Acts 1:7, 1:24, 5:4, 20:28, and 23:20).

19. It has been shown that the translation of Ephesians 4:32, "as God . . . has forgiven you," allows us to understand the forgiveness of verse 32 to be God's repetitive judicial forgiveness of believers that He provides unconditionally, time after time and day after day. It also has been shown that the context demands that we understand God's forgiveness of us in Ephesians 4:32 to be His repetitive judicial forgiveness, and our forgiveness of others in the same verse is to be unconditional *(vertical forgiveness)*.

   Further, as shown by the preceding notes, translating the aorist indicative verb in Ephesians 4:32 by the English present perfect *("as God . . . has forgiven you")* is grammatically as acceptable as translating it using the English past tense *("as God . . . forgave you")*. Some may object that no contemporary scholars were quoted, even though contemporary versions of the New Testament, such as the New King James Version, have also translated significant numbers of aorist indicative verbs by the English present perfect.

20. What does contemporary scholarship say? Even before the time of Robertson, some scholars were examining verbal systems of languages on the basis of verbal aspect as opposed to tense. Many contemporary

scholars, both linguists and grammarians, continue to study the aspectual nuances of verbs. One contemporary scholar of verbal aspect is Stanley E. Porter. In *Verbal Aspect in the Greek of the New Testament with Reference to Tense and Mood* (New York: Peter Lang Publishing, Inc., 1989), 133, Porter says:

> *[The]* aorist in Greek first and foremost indicates perfective aspect but may, though does not necessarily, implicate relative temporal reference by means of various deictic indicators. In those cases where deixis is not limited, the aorist can be used omnitemporally *[gnomic aorist seems to fall into this category]*, timelessly *[without reference to a specific time]*, as well as present and future-referring, leaving perfective aspect as the essential semantic component.

Notice that Porter says that the "aorist in Greek first and foremost indicates perfective aspect . . ." Also notice that he says, ". . . leaving perfective aspect as the essential semantic component."

21. As shown in the preceding note, Porter says that "perfective aspect is the essential semantic component" of the Greek aorist indicative. But what English verb tense reflects perfective aspect? Brinton, referring to perfective aspect in English, says, "In English, the *[present]* perfect is a verbal periphrasis consisting of a form of the auxiliary *have* and the past participle of the main verb." Laurel J. Brinton, *The Development of English Aspectual Systems, Aspectualizers and Post-verbal Particles* (Cambridge: Cambridge University Press, 1988), 10.

22. Comrie also teaches that the English present perfect translates perfective aspect. Speaking of a use of perfective aspect that he calls "Perfect of persistent situation," Comrie says, "One use of the English *[present]* Perfect, indeed one that seems to be characteristic of English, is the use of the *[present]* Perfect to describe a situation that started in the past but continues *[persists]* into the present . . . ." Bernard Comrie, *Aspect, An Introduction to the Study of Verbal Aspect and Related Problems* (Cambridge: Cambridge University Press, 1976), 60.

23. Comrie names another use of perfective aspect the "experiential perfect." Speaking of this use of perfective aspect, he says, "The experiential perfect indicates that a given situation has held at least once during some time in the past leading up to the present." Ibid., 58.

24. The English present perfect may also be used when speaking of a plurality of events that occurred in past time. For instance, consider this sentence: "He has used his paychecks *[a plurality of them, spaced at intervals in past time]* wisely."

Comrie confirms that the English present perfect can include a number of events in past time. Speaking of languages in general, but not excluding English, Comrie says, "It is quite possible for perfective forms to be used for situations that are internally complex, such as those that last for a considerable period of time, or include a number of distinct internal phases. . ." Ibid., 21.

25. Describing four categories into which uses of the English present perfect can be divided, Brinton says:

> The resultative *[present]* perfect (Type A) refers to a past situation which has present results, effects, or relevance. The continuative perfect (Type B) refers to a situation which began in the past and persists up to, and perhaps even beyond, the present. The perfect of experience (Type C) refers to a situation which has occurred once or repeatedly before the present, and the perfect of recent past (Type D) refers to a situation which occurred in the immediate past.

Brinton, *Aspectual Systems*, 10.

26. As shown by preceding quotations, (1) perfective aspect is the essential semantic component of the aorist indicative; (2) perfective aspect not only reflects completed action but also can include a plurality of events in past time; (3) the English present perfect tense accurately reflects perfective aspect; and (4) the English present perfect tense can include a plurality of events in past time.

27. Therefore, as seen by both traditional Greek grammar and by verbal aspect, translation of the aorist indicative in Ephesians 4:32 by the English present perfect *("as God . . . has forgiven you")* is every bit as valid as translating the same Greek verb by the English past tense *("as God . . . forgave you")*. The English present perfect not only reflects continuing results of His forgiveness, but also allows us to understand God's forgiveness in Ephesians 4:32 as including separate and distinct acts of His forgiveness of believers—repetitive judicial forgiveness which He graciously gives to believers time after time —the kind of forgiveness that is demanded by the context.

28. The Greek verb ἐχαρίσατο *(echarisato)* expressing God's forgiveness for us in Colossians 3:13 is the same Greek verb used for God's forgiveness of us in Ephesians 4:32. Therefore, all of the grammatical arguments presented in the preceding notes for translating this verb by the English present perfect *("has forgiven")* apply also to Colossians 3:13.

29. The New Translation—The Letters of the New Testament (Wheaton, IL: Tyndale House Publishers, 1990), 155.

Chapter Eleven—Extending the Power of Forgiveness

1. One of the problems that biblical counselors face is helping counselees become fact-oriented rather than feeling-oriented. This is especially true with regard to forgiveness—it is facts that are important for charting a course of action, not feelings.

    Counselors must not forget, however, that a counselee's feelings represent the combined effect of what others have done to him, how he reacted to them, and whether or not he has used vertical forgiveness to overcome their offenses.

    It is important, therefore, to ask counselees how they felt about an offense at the time it happened and how they feel about it now *(in addition to asking them what they have done about the offense).* To fail to inquire into the counselee's feelings, whether by design or unintentionally, is to miss vital input that God will provide through the counselee's feelings.

    And what kind of a steward is a counselor to be? If he is representing his Lord, attempting to help people find and do the will of his Lord, then he should show compassion, as did his Lord (John 11:35). How can we say that we are attempting to bring glory to Him if we appear unconcerned about the feelings of those who come to us for help? Leading counselees to be fact-oriented in their lives does not mean that their feelings should be ignored.

    Counselors, ask them how they feel about the situation now. Ask them how they felt at the time. If you don't, you are overlooking a God-given source of information—information that you need to help your counselees.

2. Releasing to God the penalty of a counselor's poor counseling does not preclude taking the problem to the local church and also warning the sheep in a circle as wide as his influence, as long as the objective is *agape* love—loving the counselor and loving the sheep that are being wounded by his counseling.

    After being confronted with the error of his ways, the erring counselor should make every effort to retract his erroneous teachings in as wide a circle as they have been distributed. But if he is unwilling to retract his erroneous teachings, loving the sheep means warning them of his errors.

3. Lenski's insight into forgiveness is helpful. Regarding Mark 11:25, he says in his commentary on the New Testament book of Mark:

    > Note the all-inclusiveness of "anything" and "anyone". . . Whether the thing be a sin in God's judgment or not, whatever it be,

as long as we hold it "against" anybody, fellow disciple or non-disciple, Jesus says: "remit it," get rid of it.

Lenski, *Mark*, 497.

Chapter Twelve—When Forgiveness "Doesn't Work"

1. When some well-meaning therapists attempt to "heal damaged emotions" by man's techniques, they look for problems that their counselees cannot remember and have supposedly repressed.

2. Whether by the power of suggestion or by hypnotism, it is dangerous to allow anyone to help you "remember" supposedly repressed memories. "Remembering" things that did not happen can damage or destroy interpersonal relationships such as parent-child relationships, can destroy reputations, and can result in prison sentences.

Chapter Thirteen—Forgive Yourself?

1. In 1 John 1:9, "confess" is translated from ὁμολογῶμεν *(homologōmen)*. If morphology accurately determined word meaning, ὁμολογῶμεν *(homologōmen)* would mean "to say the same." But word meaning is not necessarily determined by morphology. Instead, word meaning is generally determined by word usage.

   "Confess" in our culture is used with a variety of meanings ranging from absolute truth to a plea-bargained "confession" of a lesser crime than the one committed. So there is a problem establishing the meaning of the English word "confess" on the basis of word usage. In like manner, ὁμολογῶμεν *(homologōmen)* has been used throughout the centuries to convey a variety of meanings, as can be seen by reading the fourteen page discussion in TDNT, vol. 5, 199-212.

   We must look therefore to contextual usage in the Scriptures and/or theology to determine the meaning of "confess" in 1 John 1:9. And as it turns out, we can determine the meaning of the English and Greek words by theology and simple logic.

2. Does Matthew 18:23-35 teach the vertical forgiveness of Mark 11:25 or the horizontal forgiveness of Luke 17:3-4? In Matthew 18:15-17, Jesus teaches that offenders are to be confronted. The goal of confronting is to bring an offender to repentance so that he can be granted horizontal forgiveness. Jesus therefore first addresses forgiveness that is conditional—horizontal forgiveness—forgiveness that is dependent upon repentance.

   Then in Matthew 18:21-22, Jesus addresses the question of how many times an offender is to be forgiven. It is not clear by the context whether He is speaking of horizontal forgiveness, vertical forgiveness, or both. Probably **both** horizontal and vertical forgiveness are in view, since the question is **not** the conditions *(repentant or unrepentant)* nor the kind of forgiveness *(horizontal or vertical)*, but the number of times.

But does Matthew 18:23-35 teach horizontal forgiveness or vertical forgiveness? After two earlier passages in Mattew 18 that teach about forgiveness, starting with verse 23, Jesus teaches forgiveness in which the king granted forgiveness unconditionally, and in which the king expected his servant to grant forgiveness unconditionally. Therefore, it is evident that this passage teaches unconditional forgiveness *(God's repeti*tive *judicial forgiveness and our vertical forgiveness)*.

3. Jesus taught princples of rebuke and forgiveness in verses 15, 21, and 22, of Matthew 18. Then, in His illustration of Matthew 18:23-35, He teaches principles whose logic seems clear:

   - The king's forgiveness of his servant was unconditional.

   - God's repetitive judicial forgiveness of us is unconditional.

   - The king forgave his servant more than the fellow servant owed the forgiven servant.

   - God has unconditionally forgiven us more *(His repetitive judicial forgiveness)* than anyone could possibly offend us.

   - The king was just in requiring that his servant, who had been unconditionally forgiven so much, unconditionally forgive the debts of others.

   - God is just in requiring us to unconditionally release to Him the penalty of all offenses against us.

   - The king punished his servant who had been unconditionally forgiven, but who would not unconditionally forgive his fellow servant.

   - Even as the king punished his servant who would not uncondi-tionally forgive, God will chastise us if we refuse to uncondi-tionally forgive *(using vertical forgiveness)*.

4. What about the "torment" or "torture" that God brings on those who will not forgive? Does the chastisement of this "torture" or "torment" come upon those who will not forgive unconditionally, or upon those who will not forgive in response to an offender's repentance?

   Since the teaching of Matthew 18:23-35 is about forgiveness that is granted unconditionally *(without any stipulations)*, it is apparant that the teaching of Jesus' illustration parallels the teaching of Mark

11:25— the penalty of all offenses against us must be released to God unconditionally.

However, it seems reasonable to think that, since refusal to grant horizontal forgiveness to a repentant offender is rebellion against God *(even as refusal to use vertical forgiveness is rebellion against God)*, refusal to grant forgiveness to a repentant offender also could result in the torture *(chastisement)* of Matthew 18:35.

EPILOGUE

1. Lenski, *Galatians, Ephesians, Philippians*, 588-89.

2. Although Lenski did not refer to vertical forgiveness by that name, and although he did not teach that vertical forgiveness releases the penalty of the offense, he did make valuable contributions to our understanding of forgiveness.